"Social Media Rules"

By Neil Mahoney

Copyright © 2014 Neil Mahoney
All rights reserved.

ISBN: 1502825295
ISBN 13: 9781502825292
Library of Congress Control Number: 2014918693
CreateSpace Independent Publishing Platform
North Charleston, South Carolina

Dedication

To my patient, loving father, Daniel, and my patient, loving wife, Ruby, who gave me more than I can ever repay: and to my Freshman English Professor, Fr. Francis Sweeney, S. J., who set me on a path that led to an interesting, fulfilling career in Advertising, Sales and Marketing, which I wouldn't trade for anything – except my happy life with Ruby.

TABLE OF CONTENTS

Chapters:

	Introduction	vii
1	Business is War without Guns	1
2	1-Minute Management Mentality vs. SEO & Social Media	5
3	The World as It Was before Social Media	13
4	The Medium Changed. Not the Message Not the Rules.	19
5	Analyzing Wants & Needs to Optimize Market Selection	23
6	Proper Product Positioning	53
7	Branding, Inquiry Generation	59
8	Prospect Identification and Development	79
9	Why the Marketing-Sales Team Isn't really a Team	85
10	Sales: The Least Time-effective Process in all of Business	97
11	Misusing the Basics of Selling	113
12	90% Firms Don't Have a Business Plan	121
13	Smart Start Ups and Product Launches	125

14	10 Remedies for the 10,000 Pitfalls to Start Ups and New-product Launches	137
15	15 Commandments for a Truly Integrated Marketing-Sales Process	143

INTRODUCTION

When you mention Social Media to most folks over 35, they usually say, "Oh that silly stuff." This book is not about the fatuous follies of Facebook, or the twittering of twits on Twitter.

The subject we're discussing is <u>business-related</u> Social Media – both B2B and B2C. It's serious stuff -- so serious that we need to view it both as a discipline and as a developing science. Though business-related Social Media has become the dominant medium for much of Marketing Communications (MarComm):

1. It's still in an early stage of development.
2. .While Social Media is a new and different medium, it's still a form of MarComm.
3. Hence most of the tried-and-true MarComm rules still apply.

These Rules don't presume to tell Social Media pros how to produce their work, but they do suggest proven methods that will help them to:

- Identify those few major market opportunities, which you can satisfy, that present the greatest potential for optimum revenues and profits

- Create strong Branding programs that build superior awareness, perception and preference for your products or services

- Efficiently convey those messages to those <u>few, key</u> prospects and markets

- Enable Marketing-Sales to better represent your products and services to these prospects

- Maintain customer satisfaction and loyalty to foster their goodwill, which leads to repeat business and a willingness to recommend your brand to others

- Understand that Marketing-Sales is not a collection of discrete, loosely related functions, but a true process that can be readily upgraded as more important Analytics come to light

Why business needs SEO and Social Media to sell and market successfully

Today, the catch phrase "Sales & Marketing Alignment" is often seen in discussions on SEO and Social Media. Marketing-Sales pros frequently ask, "What's the difference between Sales and Marketing? Is one better than the other?" A generation ago during the Golden Age of Marketing-Sales it was clearly understood that they're complementary; they're mutually supporting; and you can't do one effectively without the other. To fully understand this you must first understand their interrelationship and interdependence.

1. Marketing's role:
   a) Using SEO, Social Media and conventional research methods, identify your key prospects based on the wants and needs your company can best satisfy.
   b) Determine the few top markets that promise optimum revenues with the best Return on Investment (ROI).
   c) Develop a short, persuasive Value Proposition that appeals to those top markets and segments
   d) Using SEO and Social Media, establish Brand Awareness and Perception, thereby generating strong product interest and prospect response
2. Sales' role:
   a) Gain an in-depth personal understanding of other specific wants and needs that individual prospects consider to be important
   b) Explain how the company can satisfy them fully and completely
   c) Provide proof of performance
   d) Build Respect and Trust
   e) Secure the sale
   f) Provide follow up to ensure customer satisfaction
   g) Alert management to Opportunities or Threats that may be detected while serving customers and prospects

Note: Virtually all the material in this book is based on my 30-plus years in all areas and at all levels of Marketing-Sales.

CHAPTER 1:
BUSINESS IS WAR WITHOUT GUNS

In war: technicians design, develop and produce the weapons that warriors use to win battles. In business: technicians design, develop and produce the products that Marketing-Sales use to win customers, and generate revenues and profits for the company.

In war, harmony and cooperation among the technicians is quite common because they have similar backgrounds and functions. But when it comes to the warriors – the ground forces, the Air Arm and the Navy – the differences are great, and must be coordinated. To accomplish these varied and difficult tasks, which are carried out by very different kinds of professionals, the military has developed a complex integrated-command structure that gathers and analyzes intelligence, then develops strategies and tactics to enable the warriors to use their weapons to maximum advantage. As General George S. Patton so aptly said, "Wars are fought with weapons, but they are won by Men."

The same is true in business. While there's commonality among the design and development teams, the dissimilarities between Sales and the several Marketing functions – Planning, Forecasting, Research, Marketing Communications and the like – differ greatly. Plus the mind-set and motivations among the various groups are also quite different. Salespeople tend to be outgoing and are, or should be, effective at describing the features and benefits of the product or service – and relating them to the wants and needs of their prospects. They're also proficient, or should be, at asking for the order and closing the sale.

Market researchers, whose role and importance have increased in this new world of Analytics, are analysts, and may or may not be outgoing and effective at meeting people they don't know. However, they are good at mining data and using formulas to project likely outcomes of actions, strategies and programs. Marketing Communications pros are usually writers and artists who understand how to create effective sales messages that capture the attention and interest of prospects, but like their fellow researchers and forecasters they're often quite unlike most salespeople.

To bring these varied and different personalities and skills to bear effectively, a business also needs an integrated command structure, typically headed by the Chief Marketing Officer (CMO) or VP of Business Development. Under their coordination the direct reports – Sales Managers, Product Managers, MarComm/Social Media Managers, etc. – are tasked to assure their organizations are proficient, well-trained and work in harmony with each other to assure strategies, plans and programs are properly developed and executed to maximize sales and profitability – plus supply key market information and new-product ideas to management to help assure the company's long-term future. It's also management's responsibility to seriously consider these ideas and not just brush them off, as happens much too often.

In my first book, "Sell Smarter, Not Harder," I discussed the several Marketing-Sales disciplines, mentioned in the following chapters, on a function-by-function basis. Here, the multi-stage process that helps optimize each function is treated sequentially to increase clarity and demonstrate the interdependence of each upon the others. In addition to emphasizing the importance of Analytics, which can now be more easily gleaned, thanks to Social Media and Search Engine Optimization, this book outlines the kinds of coordination that can and should exist among these functions in order to assure a seamless interconnection among all Marketing-Sales functions.

Traditionally, Marketing-Sales have been viewed as a series of discrete functions: Sales, Market Research, Planning, Product Management, Customer Service, Marketing Communications, etc. – all loosely connected under one umbrella, typically termed "Business Development." In fact these functions are not loosely connected. They are all integral parts of a process that begins by identifying the root of all successful business ventures: "Find, or create a need or want and fill it," and ends with sales success and a satisfied customer base.

Understanding that Marketing-Sales is truly a process, as well as a science, is essential for developing effective, coherent Marketing-Sales strategies, plans and programs, which can then be executed effectively by everyone involved in the process.

Just as war is alternatively described as an art and a science, so Marketing-Sales are both arts and sciences. During their Golden Age – the last four decades of the twentieth century – the emphasis in Marketing-Sales was on the side of art. Today, thanks to the Internet (good) and the One-Minute Management Mentality that places emphasis on immediacy and short-term results (bad), it's important that Marketing-Sales pros take advantage of practical, everyday Analytics to transform these erstwhile arts into science – and into a process that begins with:

1. Matching the benefits you provide to the wants and needs of the various markets.

2. Winnowing the many markets you can serve to the few key segments that have the potential to generate the greatest revenue for the least effort and expense.

3. Conducting a Positioning Analysis to develop a Value Proposition that clearly shows how well you meet the wants and needs of these major prospects – and in ways that set you above and apart from competition.

4. Producing sales messages that capture your prospects' attention and set the stage for follow-up action by your sales force.

The following chapters also discuss the many ways that Social Media and SEO can be used to identify the Analytics that make clear the major wants and needs of customers and prospects – those that are key to developing and conveying Marketing-Sales strategies, programs, methods and messages that will increase revenue and profits for you and your company. First, though, let's discuss why the Marketing-Sales teams often don't function as well as they should or could.

Chapter 2:
1-Minute Management Mentality vs. SEO & Social Media

Many articles on Analytics for Marketing-Sales have been published that make it seem like you need a PhD in Economics or Statistics to understand and use it. You don't – but you do need to put a lot of thought and analysis into them in order to understand your markets and what motivates your prospects to want to buy from you. This need for in-depth thought and analysis was accepted as routine during the Golden Age of Marketing-Sales, but the One-Minute Management Mentality changed all that.

The Dying Arts of Marketing-Sales

Several years ago a book, "The One-Minute Manager" became all the rage among many businesspeople. It offered short, quick remedies for dealing with business problems and situations. This unfortunately led many managers to believe that there's a quick, easy solution to everything.

In addition, two other significant developments occurred – which over several years caused a subtle but serious deterioration in the complex arts of Marketing-Sales. The developments that caused this deterioration – and now make Analytics so essential to restoring Marketing-Sales to their previous levels of effectiveness are:

1. The "Growth-share matrix concept," developed by the Boston Consulting Group. This teaches management to segment their businesses into four groups, based on market share and market growth: Stars, Question Marks, Cash Cows and Dogs. a) Stars are product lines that have high market share in high-growth markets. b)

Question Marks are lines that have moderate to low market share in high-growth markets. c) Cash Cows are lines that have high market share in low-growth or mature markets. (It's recommended that they be used to help fund the revenue that helps finance the Stars and Question Marks). d) Dogs are lines that have low market share in low-growth or mature markets and whose future value to the company is very questionable. Wisely and correctly applied this is an excellent management tool, but when used by uninformed, or impatient CEOs who put quick, easy pickings over the love of the business, the products, and their loyal employees, it becomes destructive – and many times ruinous.

2. The computer and its companion. Computer-aided Graphics enabled people who were inadequately trained in the Marketing Communications profession to produce eye-pleasing sales materials quickly, easily and inexpensively. But these messages often lacked the power and punch to sell effectively. Result: deterioration in the effectiveness of the promotional materials for many companies.

By misapplying the Growth-Share matrix, and adopting the One-Minute Management Mentality, it wasn't long before many CEOs began running their businesses on a quarter-by-quarter basis instead from decade-to-decade. This type of short-term thinking and planning led to other short cuts that saved money short term, but weakened the business long term. Here are some examples of these insidious fallacies:

1. Multi-tasking increases efficiency
2. Management is a specialty that can cut across all lines
3. Short-term managing; short-term planning

Taken one by one, here are why these are bad, self-defeating concepts:

1. Multi-tasking increases efficiency:

   A recent study on multitasking shows:
   - Tasks are almost always performed less effectively and efficiently
   - Inveterate multi-taskers have a diminished ability to focus on any one task, even when working on just one task
   - Since multi-taskers aren't able to focus as well, they don't think situations through as well

2. Management is a specialty that can cut across all disciplines:

   This has already been said, but it's worth saying again: Management skills are not enough. Truly effective managers must also possess skills and professional know-how in the functions they are managing. Effective managers must be: good critics who know good work from bad and know how to help their team fix it – plus be good teachers and good listeners. They also must be fair, impartial judges and capable defenders of their team with the courage to defend it when it's right. To do that, they must be respected and trusted by top management for skills and effectiveness. Here's one example:

   When I was a Marketing Communications Manager for a major corporation, the Division president came into my office menacingly waving a magazine and challenged me to defend why our ad was in the book. I politely told him, "Because you read it Tony." He looked surprised by the remark so I added: "We need our products to be seen by top managers like you in all the manufacturing plants." He left my office smiling.

   Here are a few more essentials to add to the list: Effective managers must also be visionary thinkers and planners, good judges of what's best for the company, and good salespeople for the department. To be an effective teacher, critic, and effective defender of the department and its work, the manager has to have mastered the craft. There's no substitute for this, as this case history shows:

Miscast Management: Many years ago I was working with a client who offered Computer Time Sharing to people who didn't have enough in-house computer resources to meet all their needs. Their marketing strategy was very well conceived: a) Engineers were technically proficient and could understand the computer. b) Engineers also had the need – Product Design & Development – so they were ideal prospects. The problem the sales force faced was, many Engineers were unfamiliar with the keyboard and needed to be encouraged to use it.

As the Adman, I was given the challenge of solving the problem. Thanks to some great Admen who came before me, they had already solved a similar challenge for a company that sold teach-yourself-at-home piano lessons. They wrote an ad that's deservedly in the Advertising Hall of Fame. The headline was, "They laughed when I sat down to play." I modified it to say, "They laughed when I sat down to compute." The accompanying photo showed a smiling Engineer happily typing away. I presented the ad at a sales meeting, and the whole room stood up and applauded. It captured the sales situation perfectly. The ad was submitted for approval and the Marketing Manager, an Engineer by training and mind-set, rejected the ad saying, "We don't make fun of our products." That's what happens when non-professionals are put in charge of specialties they don't understand.

3. Short-term management, short-term planning:

Like the Share-Growth matrix, Management by Objective (MBO) is a great concept, which has been used successfully for years, but when it's mixed with short-term planning and short-term objectives, it often becomes Mismanagement by Objective. Here are some examples:

a) Having written more than my share of Marketing Communications plans, there are many times when – out of ignorance of its full impact on the Marketing-Sales function – one of my objectives as Ad Manager was: "Increase inquiries by 10%." The objective was easily achieved: merely by running more press releases and placing more ads in cut-and-paste tabloids. But did these added inquiries do any good? I don't know, but my intentions were good, and I believed I was doing the right thing at the time. If the added inquiries weren't all that good, all I did was waste the salespeople's time and diminish their faith in the total inquiry process.

b) In magazine publishing Circulation is the life-blood of the magazine. However, maintaining and building good circulation is labor intensive. A Publisher of a magazine that competed with one of mine was given the objective: "Increase employee productivity." Calculating productivity was easy: Divide total revenue by the number of employees. The Publisher's solution: outsource Circulation. His numbers looked great that year, and he got his bonus. During subsequent years, however, the quality of his circulation degraded. He lost ad pages and the magazine eventually failed.

c) Two other case histories that demonstrate the ruinous policies that Mismanagement by Objective can cause through inept leadership are cited below. In these cases the new top managers were financial execs. Let me first acknowledge: many CFOs can and do make outstanding CEOs. However, too many CFOs, who fit Oscar Wilde's definition of cynics – "people who know the price of everything, but the value of nothing" – are made CEOs and often destroy or seriously cripple all or part of the organization.

d) Another problem that arises in relation to this focus on low-hanging fruit is that a company tends to become soft – both in terms of Marketing-Sales and in Product Development. When a company loses its competitive spirit and won't compete in areas that aren't securely in the "Star" or "Cash Cow" categories, it's not prepared to compete well when these "sweet spots" start to sour.

The MBO moral: Be careful what you ask for. You may get it.

These are just some examples of why Analytics are necessary to convert the dying art of Marketing-Sales into a science and a discipline that will restore them to their previous levels of professionalism. The following chapters discuss how to apply Analytics and Social Media to help increase the sales and profitability of companies – as well as help assure their long-term futures. But first, one more example:

What you don't know can hurt you:

To put it another way:
- If you can't or don't measure it, you can't manage it.
- If you can't manage it, it doesn't get done.

During the Golden Age of Marketing, the way B2B ad effectiveness – and the ad budgets – were measured and justified was by quantifying the number of inquiries that were generated. I used to joke that when company presidents or General Managers went to CEO school, they were taught to ask the Ad Manager one question when budget and planning time came around: "How many inquiries did we get for all the money we spent last year?"

It's gotten even sillier today. Now the Social Media Manager is asked "How many clicks and downloads did we get this year?" The reason why the question has become even sillier is because a momentary click can be nothing more than a measure of a prospect taking a passing glance at your site or posting on social media sites. This is yesterday's equivalent of a reader taking a passing glance or reading an ad or article discussing your product or service, but lacking sufficient interest to make an inquiry.

A click is by no means worthless – it helps increase brand awareness, but a download is the equivalent of a prospect – hopefully – requesting more information about that product or service. Be aware, however, that a download is not necessarily an indication of intent to buy – just an interest in the product.

Recapturing the Golden Age of Marketing-Sales

Much know-how and information has been forgotten over these past few decades due to the One-Minute Management Mentality, but it can be resurrected and maintained, as the following chapters indicate. American manufacturing resurrected itself thanks to Drs. William E. Deming and Walter A. Shewhart, who are now known as the Fathers of Quality Control today. Their views are accepted and have been adopted the world over.

Gen. George S. Patton was also a practitioner of much of their philosophy. Some of the principles he and they practiced, which are excerpted from the book, "Patton's One-Minute Messages," are repeated here:

1. The crippling disease: Lack of constancy of purpose toward improving product and service
2. Emphasis on short-term profits
3. Evaluation by performance, merit rating, or annual review of performance
4. Management by use of visible figures only – with little or no consideration of figures that are unknown or unknowable
5. Neglect of long-range planning and transformation
6. The unmanned computer. (Computers don't fix problems. They are often repositories of unused information)
7. The attitude that anyone who comes to try to help us must understand all about our business

As you read through the chapters of this book, you'll see a number of these insightful principles discussed in more detail, as well as the many ways you can use Analytics to strengthen your marketing-sales programs and messages to increase company revenue and profitability.

Chapter 3:
The World as It Was before Social Media

"Social Media Rules!!" is an acknowledgement of two facts. First, Social Media is unquestionably the dominant form of Marketing Communications today. Second, despite its dominance, it's still the offspring of printing-press-produced MarComm materials – advertising, direct mail, publicity, brochures, etc. In fact, it truly is an electronic form of MarComm.

Purely and simply, what caused Social Media to become dominant and replace the long-proven methods of printing-press-produced MarComm materials was – money, money, money.

The traditional ways of producing effective ads, direct mail, publicity, et al, were costly, but highly effective. The time, skills, effort and creativity that the process required produced many highly successful programs that resulted in increased sales and profits – not to mention great brand recognition and strong brand preference.

The reason for this greater expense was people – talented professionals working as a team. These creative teams were the main reason for the quality and effectiveness of the MarComm campaigns. Many are described throughout this book to show the level and complexity of the process. This is the same type of team effort that should be exerted for today's Social Media programs in order for them to be truly effective.

Learning to become MarComm professionals back in the Golden Age of Marketing-Sales (1960s – 1980s) – before the computer and Internet became so dominant, and before businesses were managed on a quarter-by quarter basis instead of from decade-to decade – many leading corporations conducted multi-year training programs for aspiring Admen and women.

I had the good fortune to go through one of the best – GE's Marketing Training Program. In addition to a full-time day job that was directly related to the MarComm profession, we took evening courses that were taught by in-house MarComm experts. These pros taught us all the necessary basics:

- **a)** Wants & Needs
- **b)** Strengths & Weaknesses
- **c)** Features & Benefits
- **d)** Market Research, Market Analysis & Segmentation
- **e)** Campaign Planning
- **f)** Principles of Audio Visual Production
- **g)** Effective Presentation
- **h)** And more

Here's how the process and the creative teams usually worked:

The Account Executive, often a proven-successful copywriter and an accomplished Consultative Salesperson would meet with the client-company's Ad Manager – also an experienced MarComm exec – to learn the client's business, markets and products.

Meetings would be held to learn the client's key markets and prospects, as well as the strengths of their products and the benefits they provided. Further intense discussion would usually result in what was then called the "Basic Sales Message." Now it's called the Value Proposition and it's vital that the Ad Manager and Account Exec get the essence of it right.

A good Value Proposition is a concise, persuasive, readily understood statement that highlights the key benefits that set your company and products above and apart from the competition. It clearly demonstrates how you satisfy the key wants and needs of the top two or three market segments that account for the bulk of the sales revenue in those segments. The best Value Proposition will begin with "The only ..." and will be short – 25 words or less. Once the Value Proposition has been developed and the client agrees it's the basic message they want to convey to their prime prospects, the Account Exec prepares a concise summary of the Marketing-Sales situation. The Account Exec then reviews this with the copywriter who is assigned to the account.

The Ad Copywriter: A truly skilled copywriter, who is also an experienced Adman, will have been schooled in the importance of wants and needs as they relate to persuading prospects to want to learn more about an advertiser's products by inviting a salesperson to call.

In order to do this the copywriter would sit with the Account Exec and review the client's business situation from a Marketing-Sales standpoint – key market segments, wants and needs of the prospects, and the strengths and benefits of the client's products and services vs. their competitors.

After mulling over the situation, the copywriter would work to refine and improve the Value Proposition and strategy to make them as effective as possible. Once the Account Exec approved, the copywriter would meet with the Art Director to brainstorm the theme and elements of the campaign.

The Art Director: Several times in this book I mention the "Golden Age of Marketing-Sales." Back then, Marketing-Sales skills were learned the hard way – by rote and by practice. This was especially true with Art Directors who had to learn to draw by hand and not rely on computer-aided graphics to design layouts. He or she also had to be good idea-men who could think outside the box. This is not to say today's Art Directors don't have visual talent, they do. But to prove the point, many of them are now taking courses in manual drawing and design to perfect their skills.

Returning now to the brainstorming sessions between the Art Director and copywriters, the copywriter would come into the meeting with one or two ideas to start the session rolling. Then the brain-storming session would begin. Ideas flowed back and forth until a really good one emerged. Sometimes the session would take thirty minutes or so, sometimes it took longer, but the meeting didn't end until a good idea for the headline and visual was born.

The Art Director would then prepare a layout that included the headline and visual, which was then submitted to the Account Exec for approval. Depending upon the situation, it might be decided that the copywriter would write copy for the ad or ads. Sometimes the team would wait until the client approved the campaign's concept. Either way, when the copywriter wrote the copy, the Value Proposition would occupy a prominent position. The whole package – copy, layouts, rationale for the approach, media schedule, and budget estimates were submitted for client approval.

Sound complicated does it? Well, it was involved and took time, but the creative team process bore fruit. Social Media also needs a Marketing-Sales team approach in order to be truly successful. That:

plus a thorough knowledge of the rules that make for highly successful Marketing-Sales programs. The basic rules that help assure success are outlined in the following chapters.

Chapter 4:
The Medium Changed.
Not the Message.
Not the Rules.

Back about 1970 Marshall McLuhan made the famous statement "The Medium is the Message." This can be interpreted many ways.

Today, when you ask most adults over 35, they'll often sneer, Saying Social Media is kid stuff. But for those of us who are in Marketing Communications, it is serious business. While the medium has changed from yesterday's printing- press-produced tools of persuasion, and convincing prospects that we have a real-world, money-saving solution to their business situations, we Social Media pros must convince prospects our solutions are solid. They're not Facebook fantasies or Twitter twittering.

This is where message formulation comes in – by following the tried-and-true rules of Marketing Communications. There's no avoiding them or taking short cuts.

Earlier, I mentioned that I was schooled in many of the basics of MarComm during my three years in GE's Marketing Training Program. While all the lessons learned were essential, one stands head and shoulders above the rest – creating The Value Proposition. To create a truly effective Value Proposition there are a number of steps to follow. They're the 15 Commandments for Optimal Marketing-Sales Alignment:

List all your features that have user appeal

From among them, identify the benefits you can offer to various markets and prospects

Evaluate those markets to determine which offer realistic revenue, growth and profit

Further analyze those markets to determine those few segments that offer the greatest long-term opportunity for revenue, growth, and profitability

For each of these few, key segments determine who the primary prospects will likely be – those with the greatest potential to influence the purchase your products

Having selected these few top buying-influence segments, determine their major wants and needs – the few that they most value and desire. (Some may be emotional, not rational)

From among these few, key wants and needs, determine your ability to provide them relative to competition

Carefully and realistically determine your strengths and weaknesses vs. each competitor

Once you've determined the extent of your superiority over each competitor – plus your weaknesses if any – determine those segments in which you can best compete

Having confirmed those areas where you can best compete, organize and motivate your sales organization (direct or indirect) to contact and interest those few, key prospects in your offering.

Develop a succinct (25 words or less), compelling Value Proposition that clearly sets you above and apart from the competition

Remember: a strength where you may have greater superiority over the competition, but is not as highly desired by your key prospects, may not generate as many sales as a strength where you have lesser superiority, but is considered more important by these prospects

Establish and conduct a Branding program that strongly conveys your Value Proposition

Avoid complicating it with less-important details. Let the sales force handle them

Assure that the sales force is well versed in the Value Proposition, and that they know the need to educate and motivate those prospects who are most likely to become prime customers and repeat buyers.

Social Media: A major part of the Marketing-Sales team – but still a part.

Besides demonstrating the dominance of Social Media, how it came to rule, and the rules it should follow to remain truly effective, this book's goal is to make clear that Marketing-Sales is truly an integrated process – which it has always been, is now, and ever shall be.

Social Media and SEO have added greatly to traditional marketing research methods for identifying prospects and their wants and needs. Faster and greater access to market data and the ability to communicate more quickly, effectively and efficiently – when coupled with a renewal of the insightful thought, strategy and planning that existed several years ago – is explained throughout these pages. The goal: to help Marketing-Sales professionals to

- Identify those few major market opportunities that present the greatest potential for optimum revenue and profits

- Create strong Branding programs that build superior awareness, perception and preference for your products
- Efficiently convey those messages to those few key markets and prospects

Chapter 5:
Analyzing Wants & Needs to Optimize Market Selection

Benefits, Features, Wants & Needs: The Building Blocks of Sales

We've all heard the age-old saying: "Find (or create) a need and fill it." That's the process everyone who has products or services to sell must first undertake if the business is to be successful in selling and marketing its wares. The first thing to do is to analyze and determine the markets where your product or service will have the greatest sales potential. To do that, you have to identify the benefits you offer that satisfy the wants and needs of these markets or market segments. Social media and SEO give you excellent insights into the wants and needs of many areas of the population. If your offering matches the demographics of these segments, social media, SEO and the Analytics they provide can be a great resource.

Any discussion about Marketing-Sales must include a basic understanding of:

a) <u>The benefits:</u> They are what motivate prospects to buy from you.

b) <u>The features</u> you offer: They help you prove that you can deliver the benefits you promise and that your offerings are superior to the competition.

c) <u>Wants & Needs:</u> Correctly identifying and being able to fulfill these are what motivate prospects to buy your products and/or services.

1. A benefit is a desirable effect that a product or service produces for the users of that product or service. Saving money; making a profit; improving quality; improving your looks; your health; or making things easier, faster, or better are some examples.

2. A feature is a good quality that enables a product or service to provide a benefit or satisfy a want or need. Faster operation, higher accuracy, and greater reliability are examples of such features. In most cases <u>do not</u> use a feature to imply a benefit. The feature proves the benefit. It's the benefit that motivates the prospect to buy.

3. Wants & Needs are the desires or requirements of those individuals or groups who might be attracted to any given product or service. The wants and needs of people, who will ultimately use the product or service to obtain a benefit, will vary depending upon the product or service being considered. A few examples of wants and needs are:
   - Saving money
   - Looking more appealing
   - Getting a better return on investment
   - Getting from here to there
   - Food, clothing, shelter

Learning & Satisfying Prospects' Wants & Needs:

Wants and needs are things we all have, but these vary depending upon our lifestyles, self-perceptions and work requirements. Needs are things we absolutely must have – like food, clothing and shelter – but some of those needs can also be wants. We need food and shelter, but could get these by foraging for roots and berries and living in a cave. However, very few of us want (there's that word again) to do this. You may want a McMansion and a limousine, while others might want a 4-room bungalow and a 10-speed bike. Twenty or thirty years ago few of us needed or even wanted a computer. Today, a very high percentage of us *need* at least one, while many others *want* two or more – plus a cell phone, an I-Pod, etc.

Aside from the very basics of life, wants and needs change over time. A century ago, horses, hay, a barn and a blacksmith were necessities. A stable of horses and elegant carriages were what a lot of people wanted. Today it's cars, wide-screen TVs and I-Pods.

Products, except for certain essentials, go through a seven-stage life cycle:

1. Curiosity
2. Luxury
3. Convenience
4. Necessity
5. Commodity
6. Obsolescence
7. Curiosity

They start life as Curiosities with little or no demand or market coverage, and end as Curiosities in antique shops with appeal to only a few.

Depending on the business we're in our customers and prospects all have needs – products and services they must have in order to operate efficiently and effectively. They have wants too. When you have a product or service you need or want, you explore and evaluate the options available to you.

1. As mentioned later in this section under "Analyzing & Using Market Data," Municipalities *needed* an effective, accurate way to measure the purity of water in their lakes and rivers, but they <u>wanted</u> a simple, inexpensive way to do it.

2. Railroads *wanted* a reliable, foolproof way to identify the location of their railroad cars no matter where they were – but they *needed* a system that could function under all sorts of rigorous conditions.

In every situation there'll be a small percentage of people or businesses that account for the vast bulk of the purchases, while a large majority will account for just a small fraction of the sales. Smart Marketing is all about identifying and anticipating the major wants and needs of the few top markets and market segments, then determining how to best attract those prospects and satisfy them better than the competition.

Aside from specific needs, there are certain wants that are virtually universal:
- Reliability
- Durability
- Efficiency (low operating costs)
- Low price
- Competent, fairly priced service, repair and maintenance
- Prompt, courteous response to wants and needs

There may be others that are fairly universal, but in most cases the Sales Force has been the source for individual customer-prospect wants for different products and markets. Thanks to SEO and Social Media, Marketing now has added valuable sources of these key Analytics. These opportunities should be recognized and taken advantage of as much as possible.

There are instances where wants and needs don't yet exist – or aren't readily recognized as wants or needs by prospects. A lot of people talk about Steve Jobs' comment that people don't know they have needs until a product makes them aware of them. He was referring to the many radically new innovations that are occurring in Electronics today. In truth, wants and needs have been around since Adam and Eve and the Garden of Eden. It's true, however, that people aren't fully aware they might want something until it becomes available. Here's one example:

Copy Cats

A large office-supply chain recognized that many small to mid-sized businesses used their copy facilities occasionally or quite often. To induce them to become more-frequent, more-loyal customers, they improved the appearance and utility of the area where their copy equipment was located. This not only brought in more business for their copiers, it attracted new customers, and increased the likelihood that those new customers would also shop for other office products they might want or need. This simple insight into the wants and needs of their prospects added greatly to their customer base – and to their bottom line.

The office-supply firm satisfied a want that hadn't previously been expressed or realized by their customers – a pleasant, convenient atmosphere for the many people who needed copying services – and who'd likely purchase other office-related products such as high-markup printer cartridges, cell phones and computers.

Motivating Dealers by Motivating Prospects

One very effective way to motivate dealers and build their enthusiasm (want) for your line is to create bursts of increased product interest among end-user prospects. Programs like these are common in the Consumer market but not so common in the B2B markets. We did this for a line of high-accuracy measurement systems that were used on machine tools and quality-control devices. Our product, Acu-Rite digital readout systems, already had good dealer coverage and prospect interest was already quite high. Sales were steady and growing.

To heighten enthusiasm and further build sales we decided to create a stir in the market by offering free installation on our systems for a 90-day period. We launched the program with national ads that had a whimsical theme: "Put the bite on Acu-Rite. Get free installation on all systems purchased within the next 90 days." The ads featured a cute foot-high alligator doll with a T-shirt that bore the "Put the bite on Acu-Rite" slogan. In addition to free installation customers also got the Acu-Rite alligator.

The program was a great success and created a lot of inquiries and orders. The enthusiastic response from our prospects really motivated our dealers and increased their loyalty to our line. Best of all this added motivation and goodwill lasted well beyond the 90-day period of the program.

Prompt Response to Needs & Requests

Another want that prospects have, but seldom voice is their desire for "Prompt Response to Needs and Requests." When I was publisher of a Manufacturing Management magazine, an Association that rep- resented dealers who served these prospects asked me to conduct a Survey to determine what features – other than product attributes such as accuracy and reliability – were most desired when considering purchases.

To the surprise of many, "Prompt Response to Needs and Requests" ranked a very strong second, just below Low Price, which ranks at the top in almost every survey. What came in third wasn't even close. Prompt Response costs a company very little, if anything, and is not Rocket Science. Yet it's surprising how many salespeople and companies overlook this highly important, seldom-stated customer want.

Gathering Market Intelligence & Selecting Markets:

The products and/or services you offer, and the user benefits they provide, dictate the markets and prospects you can serve. The trick is to identify those markets and prospects – as well as their major wants and needs. Accurate market identification is key to any company's success. It's the only way to generate substantial revenue for you and your company – as well as the best return on investment – and it isn't easy.

Thanks to the Internet this world of Analytics is now largely at your fingertips. You can mine it for:

- Data on market size and sales volume using Bing, Google, or other search engines – but bear in mind that data based on published price lists are most-often overstated because actual pricing is often lower. Also, market sizing based on Association data can be overstated because the larger companies tend to be over-represented. Smaller companies frequently choose to shun the added membership costs. While Social Media and SEO have become sources for Analytics for all sorts of prospects, be careful and selective as to how you use this data.

- Yellow Page listings: local, regional, or national: Except for rare occasions, businesses will have a listing in the local Yellow Pages. In some instances duplications of listings in neighboring areas occur. Where they don't, however, the national-listings will give a reasonably accurate total. Golf Driving Ranges is one example.
- SIC listings, targeted by broad or specific business categories. (Several years ago the government changed the SIC designation to NAICS, but it's the same listing and most people still refer to it as SIC.) The codes can be as specific and as long as eight or more digits, or as short and as broad as two. The total number of companies and number of plants will usually be included. For company size and dollar sales, you'll want to access specific company listings.
- Company listings, such as Moody's, Bloomberg's Business Week and Dun & Bradstreet: these are available on the Internet and in almost all major libraries. The volumes in the library usually have more-detailed information.
- Product listings, such as the Thomas and Sweets catalogs: Again, these are posted on the Internet, which the catalogs that provide national data have moved to. Local and state directories are still available in most libraries.
- Known prospects – again, for companies the Internet and the directories mentioned above can supplement any information you may have.

Analyzing & Using Market Data

Analyzing market data can be very tricky. As mentioned above, data can be easily misinterpreted because much of the published information can be incomplete, understated or overstated, leading you to conclude that the market size is smaller or larger than it really is, and revenues are greater or lesser than they really are. If at all possible, confirm your assessments by contacting an industry consultant or someone familiar or involved with the industry.

Don't forget the Sales Force – and the SWOT Analysis

While the sales force probably won't be able to give you good over- all information on market size and opportunity, they will be able to give good insights on the wants and needs of specific customers and types of customers. Their insights can often help you avoid pitfalls that are hidden or absent from general market data. Some of the case histories cited below demonstrate this. Sales will also be able to tell you about the competition and what they're doing. Salespeople hear a lot about the competitors' strengths every day from customers and prospects who are only too glad to let them know their offerings aren't the only choice out there.

Don't expect the sales force to do all your research for you, however. When it comes to Opportunities and Threats (the O and the T in SWOT), that's primarily the job of Senior Management – especially the CMO. Opportunities and Threats are also where Analytics, derived from Social Media and SEO, are particularly helpful. Opportunities often lie right under your nose, but you have to think outside the box to see them. Related markets and indirect influences can often be great sources for increased revenues and profits, if they're properly exploited. Much more is said about this later. Threats are often harder to detect than Opportunities. Several years ago, no one would have thought that computer screens would replace books and magazines. No one would have thought that lasers would make hand-held high-precision measurement tools a thing of the past. No one would have thought that people would spend much of their day texting and talking on cell phones – plus using them to get answers to all their questions.

Mixed blessings

All the information that's now available electronically is both a boon and a bane. Information is so prevalent you can find answers to almost anything. The real danger is that so much information is available that you have to know when to stop gathering it, or have a system that lets you separate the wheat from the chaff. Don't react to every factoid. Wait until it's been proven valid – or sufficiently prevalent. This is true whether it's for wants and needs, strengths or weaknesses, or opportunities or threats.

Pareto's Curve

Just about every business, be it product or service, has two or three market areas, market segments, or types of users that account for most of the industry's sales – in dollars, units, or otherwise. This phenomenon is so well established and universal that it's been given a name: "Pareto's Curve." The curve is named after an Italian mathematician and economist who lived around 1900 AD. He discovered that 20% of the population had 80% of the wealth, and this concept has proven itself valid time after time, market after market.

In analyzing market data it's very important to remember that Pareto's curve is not a rule, but is a rule of thumb. It's also sometimes called the 20-80 rule or a hockey stick because the curve runs slightly upward for about 80% of the distance along the X axis, then turns sharply upward for the remaining 20% of the distance. By using Pareto's curve you can identify really important segments of any market – those that account for the lion's share of the business.

Very few markets or market segments follow Pareto's curve exactly, but it's used by professionals to depict the big market opportunities they know exist – or most-likely exist. From these, market planners formulate strategies and programs by identifying key prospects and prioritizing their wants and needs in order to develop strong, persuasive sales messages – as well as deciding the most-effective, efficient ways to reach and serve them.

The US market for hardware and hand tools provides an excellent example. It is a huge market and is both B2B and B2C. This market has about 90 million purchasers per year. They are categorized as Light Do-It-Yourselfers, Moderate & Serious Do-It-Yourselfers, and Professional Contractors.

    a) Light Do-It-Yourselfers account for about 70% of all the buyers in the market, but they account for only 20% of the dollar purchases (Pareto's curve again). These are the people who keep a pair of pliers and a screwdriver in their kitchen drawer, for example. They're expensive to market to because of their vast number, low-dollar purchases, and the many and varied retail outlets they buy from.

    b) Moderate & Serious Do-It-Yourselfers account for almost 25% of the purchasers and about 25 to 30 percent of all sales. Serious DIYers like to emulate the Professional Contractors and often buy the brands the Pros use. Both Moderate and Serious DIYers like to shop at the big-box Home Improvement chains. While this makes establishing market coverage easier, to get these chains to carry your products you have to demonstrate brand acceptance or give large discounts before they'll take on your brand.

c) Professional Contractors account for no more than 5% of all purchasers, but more than 50% of all dollar sales. They demand top quality and ruggedness because they're very hard on their tools. They push them to the limit to get the job done as quickly as possible – time is money. They also buy most of their tools and hardware supplies from Contractor Supply Houses, which specialize in serving the Pros.

Stop, Look & Listen:

Be very careful when you're analyzing markets and market segments. Errors in these areas can cost you and your company dearly. Here are some examples:

1. A start-up company was financed by a group of Venture Capitalists, who didn't do a thorough job of due diligence. The market price of competing products was greatly overestimated because they relied solely on published price sheets. It wasn't until the product – which had marginal superiority over the competition – was launched and participation in industry trade shows was undertaken. After talking with both prospects and competitors at the show, it was quickly learned that true market pricing for the product was about one-third the amount shown on published price sheets. The cost of producing the new, slightly superior product couldn't be sufficiently reduced to make it competitive in the market.

2. A large, international company that manufactured scientific instruments thought they saw a great opportunity when the US became increasingly aware of pollution and its impact on the

environment. The well-known company, which manufactured spectrophotometers that were used to analyze chemicals and particles in liquids, immediately began a program to develop a miniaturized spectrophotometer that had the capabilities of their full-sized models. After funding this development and proving the mini-model's capability for conducting the analysis, it was discovered that towns, cities and other municipalities had devised a less-costly method for conducting the analysis. They gave lower-paid workers, who had drivers' licenses, bottles. They had them visit lakes, streams and rivers, fill the bottles, drive them back to the testing lab, and give them to trained personnel for analysis.

3. A major worldwide company I worked for correctly identified the wants of the railroad industry, but failed to fully recognize its needs: Result, a multi-million dollar fiasco that befell one of its divisions. The division was developing an automatic rail- road-car identification system that promised to be superior to car-identification systems then in use. They developed an electronic device that could be suspended under each car to report that car's location in any kind of weather. It looked like a great idea, but:

Mistake #1: A young non-technical trainee copywriter who was writing a sales brochure for the system noticed that the electronic black boxes were hung below the axles of the cars and were susceptible to damage by large objects, such as rocks, that might be on the tracks. He called my attention to it and I called the client. The division design engineers went back to their drawing boards and after much time and expense fixed the problem – or so they thought. The system was tested on the Union Pacific and passed with flying colors.

a) <u>Mistake #2:</u> A second test was conducted in Canada. In cold climates like that they have things called "de-icing sheds" to melt snow and ice that has accumulated on the railroad cars. The extreme heat from the sheds ruined the black boxes. Result: No product.

b) <u>Mistake #3:</u> Even worse, this giant corporation also manufactured diesel engines for railroads. That division had all the market knowledge anyone would ever need. No one bothered to talk with the experts in the diesel engine division.

The moral: Don't just analyze the overall market data; analyze the intricacies of the market before you jump in.

Know When to Stop:

In other words, use the KISS principle. One of the dangers with all the information available on the Internet and Social Media – plus today's emphasis on Analytics – is that it makes the tendency to over-analyze so easy. The secret to success has long been the KISS principle: "Keep it simple, stupid"

- Know the top two or three market segments that account for the large bulk of your sales and focus on them
- Know the top two or three wants and needs that your customers and prospects value most and emphasize them

Be satisfied with concentrating on that. Beyond that, you're just making added work for yourself, your sales force, and the Marketing Communications staff, that has to develop and promote your Value Proposition, Elevator Pitch, website and promotional materials. The more elements you add to the equation, the more complex, and expensive you make things for everyone – including your customers and prospects and dealers.

When the number of elements is increased, the complexity of the situation increases geometrically. It's easy to say that a second or third option is a small increase. But when you add that third option the complexity of marketing and selling it rises by 6X. When you add the fourth, the complexity of marketing and selling it rises by 24X. It's nice to be able to offer lots of choices, but your offer makes things much harder for everybody – including your customers and prospects. Plus you greatly increase your sales expense and reduce profitability.

<u>Get out and see the world.</u> Marketing people – especially those in large corporations – need to resist the urge to sit behind their desks or in their cubicles and crunch numbers. They should get out and see the real world by making joint calls with the sales force. Make calls with several of them: not just one or two. Between calls, ask the salespeople questions and get their perceptions and side of things. This will make the Analytics you gather much more understandable and meaningful.

This is not to say Analytics shouldn't be examined and studied continually in depth. The ever-growing body of Analytics, and the insights they provide into the wants and needs of your prospects, can provide you with ideas on how you can improve or create new products or services that can generate added revenues and profits.

Analytics are a great and growing tool – a tool that's unequalled in its value and helpfulness. Before this data became available, companies would have had to invest many thousands of dollars in order to replicate – or even conceive – the ideas and opinions that Social Media are providing on a day-to-day basis. Best of all, it's free for the taking – but be selective, be objective, and be very careful in the data you use.

Indirect Influences – Often Forgotten But Never Gone

In the Consumer market indirect influences are everywhere: Parents influence children; children influence parents; Dentists suggest the type of toothpaste and toothbrush to use; at the supermarket you often buy an alternate brand if yours isn't there. Indirect influences affect our behavior almost everywhere we turn.

In the world of B2B, indirect influences are less obvious, but they're there – and there are plenty of them. Virtually every market is made up of various market segments that have different wants and needs, as well as characteristics that conform to the 20/80 rule of thumb:

- A large number of small, relatively inexperienced users who account for a small percent of the spending
- A small number of heavy users who are quite knowledgeable and account for most of the spending

The key is to learn your market and know the customers and indirect influencers who can influence the sale. Earlier, we recapped the giant Hardware/Hand-tool market, which consists of about 90 million purchasers a year. We also mentioned the Construction Pros, who are only about five percent of the purchasers but account for over 50 percent of the spending. Selling to them is vital, but helping retailers sell profitably to the 70 percent who buy just 20 percent requires special thinking too.

Making it easier for retailers to sell to the 70% who buy only 20%

The Marketing VP of a large, well-known manufacturer of hand tools, fasteners, fixtures, hinges, etc. – all the little things people have around the house, but aren't sure how to install or use because they've never done it before, and will not do it again any time soon – came up with a brilliant solution that made selling much easier and less time consuming for retailers who served these not-so-profitable customers.

His simple, but brilliant solution to the retailers' headache was to place short, clear, how-to instructions on the backs of the blister packs that held the item stocked on the retailers' shelves. (Everybody does it today, but not back in the 60s.) Besides being a great help for the customers, it saved store personnel countless hours of repetitive explanation. The manufacturer not only increased sales and gained the goodwill of the end users, but also gained market coverage from the thousands of retailers that flocked to their brand.

Residential Construction

When a house is built, most suppliers of building materials focus on the Building Contractor. But before the house can be built, it must be designed and the materials and equipment specified. That's the job of the Architect who specifies everything – from the foundation to the rooftop. Because most specifications for houses and buildings contain an "or equal" clause, the General Contractor becomes a major influencer of the materials and systems used in the construction – but only with the Architects' permission, which they almost always give, There are many more indirect influences, however.

- The Electrician & the Mason
- The Plumber & the Roofer
- The Landscaper
- The Realtor

All want to offer the best product they can for the lowest possible price to the prospective buyer. There are also many Contractor Supply Houses and other types of dealers involved, so the numbers of indirect influences are many and varied. That's why it's important to analyze and understand the markets and their many facets when you're trying to sell your products or services.

Commercial Buildings & Tenants – cover all the bases

Office buildings, warehouses, factories, hospitals, and apartments and condominiums present sales opportunities that are similar to the Residential market. They need paint, floor coverings, etc. The type and color are often left to the tenants, so it's important to contact them. In some instances the building owners, themselves, will be involved. In any case it's smart to establish relationships with them, if possible, and with managers, and the Maintenance staffs. They often have a say-so or have strong influence on the sale.

Don't forget the really big elephant upstairs

For a large building-construction project in Texas a not-so-well known manufacturer of air-conditioning systems was specified and approved by all the usual buying influences – the Mechanical Contractor, the Maintenance Department and the Facilities Manager. The A/C manufacturer was also the low bidder to the tune of almost $20,000.

They had everything going for them except one thing. The one thing was the building's owner, a very large real-estate firm located in Chicago. The reason why the low bidder lost the business was because the owner wasn't familiar with the A/C manufacturer and his brand. The owner didn't want an "unknown" brand in his building. It all came down to his wanting to project an image of top quality for every facet of his "Class A" property, which was to be marketed for top rental fees. As it turned out, the A/C manufacturer hadn't covered all the bases in the approval process and learned the lesson the hard way.

Sometimes Needs and Wants Are in Conflict

Some of the earlier case histories illustrated that proposed solutions to many prospects' needs often don't correspond with their wants. There are also many cases where their wants will be in conflict with their needs. While these conflicts may seem unreasonable, they're nonetheless real and aren't easy to overcome. In many cases the best solution is time.

One such real-world example is a Plant Manager who bought an expensive machine tool that wasn't accurate. He brought in a Quality Control expert who used a simple method that clearly demonstrated the problem. The Plant Manager refused to accept the results – and the QC expert's relatively inexpensive solution. It took a while, but the Plant Manager finally admitted to himself that the expensive lemon he had bought was at fault and what he wanted to be true; wasn't. He took the QC expert's advice – and made the small investment that solved the very expensive problem.

Here's another example that demonstrates the importance of emotion overriding logic. In this case it involves different levels of buying influences, but the outcome was very much the same – emotion still overruled logic.

Night vs. Day

Back in the mid 1960s a worldwide industry giant that's recognized as a leader in all types of lighting developed a new type of lamp for streetlights. The lamps emitted a vivid orange glow, so that streets with that type of lighting seemed bright as day – even though it was pitch-black night. Everybody – the utilities, city officials, store owners, etc. – were excited by the new concept. As a consequence, many streets were given this type of lighting. There was just one hitch: No one bothered to ask Mr. or Ms. John Q. Public if they wanted their night turned into day.

They didn't. That's why so few streets in the US have that bright, orange glow at night – despite the advantages of lower cost of operation and greater safety. When it's night, people want it to look and feel like night.

Other related Buying Influences: Distributors & Dealers

Distributors and Dealers can be a very important part of a company's sales strategy and success – if the company takes the time to learn their wants and needs – and knows how to manage and motivate them correctly.

Though they're rarely thought of this way, distributors and dealers are usually the company's best customers. They not only buy the company's products, they stock and sell and sell them as well, so in addition to being the manufacturer's best customers, they help reduce inventory cost. Also, by maintaining local stock they help assure prompt delivery, which ranks very high on the wants and needs of virtually all customers and prospects. What's more, they can multiply a company's sales presence by forty-fold or more. Plus, that manufacturer's bad-debt ratio is usually lower than manufacturers that sell direct.

You don't get something for nothing, however. There are costs involved. Typically, a distributor that stocks, inventories and services a company's products will earn a 25 or 35 percent discount. For those distributors that don't stock because of the large size or complexity of the system, the discount is less – usually about 15 percent.

To be successful in selling through distributors and dealers, there are four things you must do: Manage them. Motivate them. Train them. Select them wisely.

1. <u>Manage them:</u> Many manufacturers make the assumption that when they appoint a distributor or dealer to sell their line, it's the sole responsibility of that distributor or dealer to do the selling. This is most often not the case. It's important to realize that they are not your employees – they are your selling partners, and have other lines to sell. Many times they'll be more comfortable with the lines they've carried for a while, or their other lines may be more important to them from a profit or customer-service standpoint. Let them know that you care about their success and welfare almost as much as they do. It's not just the responsibility of your sales force to earn their loyalty and trust, it's important that they know that management is interested and involved as well. Occasional visits from management are important, but it's also important that they believe you're actively involved in helping them develop the business and the profitability of the line for them.

2. <u>Motivate them:</u> First and foremost: Make them buy and stock your products. Once they know you require all distributors to buy and stock, they'll have confidence that low-overhead operators won't be around to undercut them. Another excellent way to motivate them is by conducting end-user promotional programs such as special discounts or product tie-ins that offer added value. This is a "pull" strategy. It often works much better than the overused "push" strategies. Push programs – loading dealers with merchandise – often backfire because dealers choke on the excess inventory and get turned off on the line instead of wanting to sell it. Opportunities for them to increase profit or win prizes based on performance are also effective motivators.

3. <u>Train them:</u> It's your product they're carrying and they'll never know your line as well as you and your salespeople do. They do know their customers and prospects much better than you do, however, so train them in the areas that will help them better serve their market area. Part of the discount they earn is for providing basic product service – not sophisticated equipment overhaul. Train them in the basics so they can earn the discount you're providing.

4. <u>Select them wisely:</u> Even companies that are well known and have great reputations don't recruit every distributor or dealer they want. More often than not, they'll have all the responsibility they can handle – both from a personnel and an investment standpoint. No matter what your reputation and market stature, you can expect to be rejected more often than not. Just as companies and salespeople rank markets and prospects A, B, and C, so do distributors and dealers based on the markets they serve. Averages show that they devote 72 percent of their time and effort to the lines they rank "A," 25 percent to lines they rank "B," and only three percent to those they rank "C." So be very sure that the ones you select rank your line at least a "B."

Consultants:

Consultants are often important buying influences too so don't overlook them. The company that goes to the expense of utilizing their services values their advice and expertise. If at all possible, learn who they are and don't ignore them or their potential influence. They'll vary depending upon the type of customer. Here's a partial list:

- Advertising Agencies
- Website Designers
- Publicists, SEO Specialists
- IT Specialists
- CPAs
- Investment Advisors
- Human Resource Services
- Lawyers

Related Markets & the Market-Segment Sidestep

So far, this discussion has shown the nuances and surprises that most markets – if not all – await the unsuspecting businessperson. This section on market segmentation shows how you can take advantage of these nuances to increase revenues and profits with little added effort or expense.

The Market-Segment Sidestep:

Pareto's Curve or the 20/80 Rule was discussed earlier. Market segmentation is a refinement of that by which you analyze segments within a larger market. The analysis of the Hardware/Hand Tool market, previously described, illustrates that clearly. Sidestepping into related segments often lead to opportunities for added sales with little extra effort or expense. The case histories cited here are just a few examples. There are many, many more market segments that offer such opportunities.

The Building Contractor Sidestep

A manufacturer of precision measuring equipment, which included hand tools such as micrometers and calipers, decided to enter the large and complex hardware market. To do this, it was evident:

1. It would take several years and several million dollars to establish brand awareness and preference among the millions of prospects in just the US, alone.

2. It would require hiring, training, and funding a second sales force to build adequate market coverage among the thousands of retail outlets that serve all those prospects.

By studying the markets more closely they decided that market segmentation might hold the key to success, both long and short term. In the hardware-hand-tool market there are three major segments, as discussed above: a) Light Do-It-Yourselfers, b) Moderate and Serious Do-It-Yourselfers, c) Professional Contractors

Because the company already served the manufacturing pros in the industrial sector, they not only had a good reputation for top quality and durability, they also had solid distribution among Supply Houses where the Contractor Pros also bought most of their tools and materials. Good market research and market segmentation helped assure their success just by sidestepping into the Contractor Professional market segment, which accounted for more than half of all sales in the hardware hand-tool market.

Mastering the Sidestep through Market Research

To identify your best opportunities for executing a successful market-segment sidestep, you need market research – guessing and speculation won't do it. There are two kinds of market research:
- Primary research is research you initiate – through interviews with individual customers and prospects, and/or with focus groups made up of several knowledgeable people who

are representative of the market. When doing this research it's very important that you use a reliable expert to conduct it. It's also important that the people sampled represent a true cross-section of your markets or market segments, and that the questions they are asked will elicit their true beliefs. The way questions are phrased can greatly influence results. For example: if you ask people what they "think" about something, you'll get a very different answer than if you ask them how they "feel" about something.

- Secondary research is research that already exists. Search engines and the Analytics that are now available through Social Media make this easy to do, but you want to be sure the research you use accurately reflects your markets – and that it was done well. Much research that purports to size markets on a revenue basis is based largely on published price sheets. Today, especially, price sheets seldom reflect actual pricing.

Despite the terminology, you usually do secondary research first and the primary research second. When you're analyzing your situation and opportunities, it's essential that you look at each and every market segment – not just the general market category, or those segments the company presently serves. Consider all segments you might be able to serve effectively.

When conducting primary research it's very important to get a "projectable" response from prospects in order to draw fairly accurate conclusions from the results. At minimum, 85 completed returns from the questionnaires you send out are required for the results to be considered projectable. The percent of returns is also a factor, but for practical purposes, let's just stick with the simple numbers.

The way you phrase the questions you ask also can affect the outcome of the research. Unless you're relatively skilled at crafting research questionnaires, you should ask a professional for help.

Sidestepping into related segments or markets can often be done fairly easily and inexpensively, as the following examples show:

The Commercial Building Sidestep

Commercial Buildings are a very large, multi-billion dollar market in the US. As of the year 2000, there were about 6.4 million buildings that totaled 85 Billion square feet – more area than the entire area of the state of West Virginia, and almost as much square footage as the US residential market in total. What's more, 65% of it is very similar to the residential market as it relates to user wants and needs.

Despite its immense size the commercial building segment is often overlooked by companies, which provide similar products and services to the residential market. Examples of these are Interior Decorators, Plumbers, Electricians and other service providers – plus manufacturers and dealers that sell paints, carpeting, etc.

Once a company establishes itself in the Commercial Buildings market, their sales and marketing costs are often substantially reduced long term. However, this market usually involves a greater sales and marketing effort to begin with, and volume discounts can reduce selling prices somewhat. To enter this market companies should first establish relationships with the Facilities Management and Maintenance staffs. This will gain them access to the tenants, who most-often are the end users. However, the building owners and managers, themselves, are often the end users, so they're good prospects as well.

The Building Rentals Sidestep

Here's a real-world example of how opportunities were almost lost by failing to take advantage of another huge, often-overlooked market segment. A magazine that published news and information on Commercial Building activities in a large southern city did an outstanding job convincing building owners and managers that they could promote the availability of their rental space by advertising to prospective business tenants who might want to relocate. The ad revenue from that segment was substantial, but it had peaked, and wasn't enough to keep the magazine sufficiently profitable.

Upon further analysis, we found a related market that was ready and waiting – one that promised more potential advertisers and advertising revenues than could be gotten from the building owners, themselves. This related market opportunity was the demand for products and services that's created when businesses relocate – moving furniture and equipment, buying new office furniture and equipment, setting up new computer networks, redecoration, etc. The list of prospective advertisers was long and promising. By inviting the companies that supplied these products and services to advertise, the magazine would generate enough revenue to make it quite profitable.

Too Much of a Good Thing

There's a danger in overdoing the Market Segment Sidestep. Creating too many niches or choices can make things too complicated or confusing for the prospects and the retailers and dealers who serve them. A well-known clothier created so many variations of their men's shirts that their outlets were frequently out of their more-popular styles, and the sales clerks wasted so much of their and their customers' time that customers stopped shopping there. There are too many instances like this to try to list them all, but food, beverages, and restaurant menus are a good place to start.

The Laffer curve

Back during the Reagan Administration the Laffer curve, also known as Supply-Side Economics, was used to demonstrate the efficacy of reducing tax rates to increase tax revenue. Illustrated by turning a bell curve turned on its side, it demonstrates that in every situation there's an optimum point where you can maximize revenue and profits. If you overdo things – too many customer options, too many competing dealers in an area, too high a tax rate, etc – you start losing revenue and profits. It's all based on the simple concept of motivation and de-motivation. If you make things too complex people will get frustrated and look for simpler ways to satisfy their wants and needs.

Niche Marketing

At the beginning of the discussion on Indirect Influences it was mentioned that the consumer market had indirect influences almost everywhere you turned, hence this chapter would not be complete without at least a few words about niche marketing as regards the B2C markets. Today, with the broad selection of Cable Television stations, a company can target its message by:
- Age group
- Income group
- Political preference
- Special interests, such as cooking, gardening, etc.
- Sports interests
- Men

- Women
- Children

In addition, Social Media such as Twitter, Facebook, and LinkedIn offer access to people who have many different types of education and interests. The choices are almost endless, and the same is true with radio and print media – most newspapers can target prospects by zip code or neighborhood. You can also make a big splash by using blimps or planes trailing banners overhead. A company can also impress prospects by using television to reach out-of-town conventioneers or trade-show attendees in their hotel rooms. We did that at one trade show in Chicago. The attendees were surprised to see our company's B2B product shown on consumer TV. They flocked to our booth and commented on how impressive it was to see an industrial product broadcast in their hotel rooms. Even though you can buy 30-second spots in major cities for about $500, when people see your ad on TV, they assume it's national and are really impressed. One thing to remember: When trying to reach out-of-town prospects at special events, appealing to their wants and needs isn't as important as promoting your brand. The main purpose is to make prospects aware that you're there, and get them to visit you.

Chapter 6:
Proper Product Positioning

Positioning was the word used during the Golden Age of Marketing-Sales to describe the multi-step process that must be used to develop what's now called the Value Proposition. Whatever you call it, you can't properly develop these Sales & Marketing materials without it:

- Elevator Pitches
- Mission Statements
- Ad Campaigns
- Slogans
- Publicity
- Websites
- Brochures, etc.

Positioning isn't easy. It takes a lot of critical thought and analysis, but once you've got it right, everything else comes easy. Once you've done your homework on wants and needs and market selection, based on the research you've done via Analytics, Primary and Secondary research, interviews with customers, and input from the Sales Force, you're ready to begin the Positioning process, which is a synthesis of what you've determined to be:

a) Your top markets and prospects, including key buying influences – direct & indirect
b) Their major Wants & Needs
c) Your Strengths & Weaknesses vs. the competition

d) Matching your proven strengths to the major wants & needs of your key buying influences

Not until you've completed this process are you ready to develop and perfect your Value Proposition. If possible, the best Value Propositions will begin with "The only . . ." and won't be more than 25 words long. Here's how it's done:

Step 1: Identify your two or three top markets and prospects, the few that account for the bulk of all your sales. By limiting your list to these top prospects, you'll keep focused on the relatively few users who account for most all your sales. This not only helps to optimize sales and marketing costs, it helps reduce design and production expenses because you'll stay focused on what's really important to your major prospects and won't be distracted by details that don't add that greatly to sales and profits. Here's one example:

What do you want for a quarter?? Business has a term for strategic cost cutting: Value Engineering – and it's broken the hearts of many Design and Manufacturing people. My first assignment on GE's Marketing Training Program was with a division that made fan motors. GE had perfected a motor that could run every minute of the day, every day of the year, for 25 years with no maintenance or lubrication whatsoever. Everyone in the division was really proud of this motor. It was one of the reasons why GE could boast of the long life of its refrigerators. However, consumer research revealed that people in the US didn't keep refrigerators that long any more – eight years was the average time owners kept them before buying a new one. It was decided that it was better business to build refrigerators that would run reliably for 12 years and sell them for less.

Our matchless 25-year motor cost 25 cents more than another motor we made that was proven to operate reliably for 12 years. The refrigerator people opted to save the 25 cents and pass the savings on to the customer. A quarter here, a quarter there, and pretty soon you're talking about a lot of happy customers.

Step 2: Once you've determined the wants and needs of your top prospects, evaluate your ability to satisfy those wants and needs in relation to your competition. Then determine your major selling points (benefits supported by features) based on this analysis. Prioritize these proven and demonstrable strengths according to the wants and needs of your top markets and prospects.

Always remember: A highly important customer benefit in which you have lesser superiority over competition – but are still superior – will likely generate more sales than a benefit where you dominate the competition, but is less-important to your prospects.

Step 3: Once you've done all this you're now prepared to develop your short, convincing positioning statement or Value Proposition. This statement may change depending upon the type of prospect you're trying to sell. For example: Managers may be better persuaded by return on investment (ROI) data, while Product Designers may be better persuaded by ease of use, or better design capabilities.

Because SEO and Social Media make so much customer-prospect information available today, beware of the strong tendency to complicate your Value Proposition with too many motivators that may be marginal to your basic sales message. Focus on the top two or three motivators that give you the greatest competitive advantage among those few segments or prospects that promise the best revenue opportunities and the best ROI.

Step 4: When the statements have been polished to perfection, circulate them among Sales and Management to get buy-in from all parties. Once you've gotten agreement, use it everywhere you can: Mission Statements, Elevator Pitches, Advertising, Publicity, Social Media, Websites, and sales materials of all kinds. The first Value Proposition you develop won't be the best. A truly effective Value Proposition requires a lot of thought and understanding of the market and prospects to get it perfected – for example:

Is it a cleaner that disinfects, or a disinfectant that cleans?

This case history illustrates perfectly that what a company thinks will best motivate the customer isn't always right. About 30 years ago a large, well-known manufacturer of household products developed the first household cleaner that could both clean and disinfect bathrooms, kitchens, and other places around the home. They debated whether the product should be marketed as a "Cleaner that disinfects," or a "Disinfectant that cleans." They chose the latter because the product's ability to disinfect was their exclusive. Sales did fairly well, but the product didn't take the market by storm.

A while later, they analyzed the wants and needs of the market more thoroughly, and they discovered that while prospects wanted both, most of them felt that a cleaner was more important than a disinfectant. The manufacturer changed the product's positioning from "A disinfectant that cleans" to "A cleaner that disinfects." This simple but important change caused the market to really react. Sales zoomed.

Bigger is better

When I became a magazine publisher, my first assignment was to turn around a digest-sized Manufacturing Management magazine, which had lost almost half of its business in less than 2 years. Because digest-size magazines are smaller than the more widely desired full-size magazines, they must have larger circulations to compete effectively for the advertisers' business. I spent the first five months making calls with the sales force and we were beginning to make some headway – too little in my opinion, but management seemed fairly pleased. Flying back from a trip one day, it hit me!! "Start thinking like the customer" I told myself. When I had been on the Ad Agency side, the larger circulations and added market reach that digest-size magazines offered were what offset the disadvantages of smaller size. If we coupled full size with our superior circulation, I reasoned, we'd take the market by storm.

I made the suggestion to my boss, the president of the division. He then took it to his boss, the president of all the ABC publications. They both liked the idea but were concerned that if my idea bombed, the magazine would go under. My boss' boss smiled sardonically and said, "If you think you can really pull it off that's fine, but if you don't, it's your job."

We pulled it off – big time. In less than 18 months after upsizing and raising our rates, we had doubled our sales and 80 percent of the revenue went right to the bottom line. I not only got to keep my job, but got a healthy raise as well,

What does this have to do with positioning and Value Propositions?? When we upsized the magazine and kept our superior circulation, here's the powerful Value Proposition we were able to tell our prospects: "We are the only full-size magazine that thoroughly covers the two most-important, heavy-user segments in the industry: Large high-volume manufacturers and Contract Manufacturing businesses."

"The only" in a Value Proposition really commands attention, and puts you in a competitive position all by yourself.

57

Pigeonholes

The reason why positioning statements and Value Propositions are so essential is that the way we remember things is by slotting information into our brain's memory banks, which are like pigeonholes in a desk. When we learn something we want to remember – say cars – we put it in our mental pigeonhole for cars. We've got Chevvies there, Fords, Rolls Royces – everything. When the Prius came out and we thought a gas-sipping car was great we put it at the top of the pile in our pigeonhole. We do that with everything – mops, brooms, floor cleaners, clothes, tailors – everything. So when you introduce a new or improved product, you're asking your prospects to put your information – or the impression you want to leave them with – in one of their pigeonholes.

If your prospects haven't yet established a mental pigeonhole for your product category and you want them to remember some fact, they have to create that pigeonhole, and as the supplier of that product or service that takes more work on your part. That's the bad news.

The good news is that you now own that pigeonhole and that special part of their minds – until other competitors come along and induce them to put their information in that pigeonhole too. What they keep on top is called "brand preference" and all marketers want that. That's why they keep promoting and "improving" their products or services – so they can stay at the top of the memory-preference pile. To paraphrase General MacArthur: Those that don't just slowly fade away – or end up on the bottom shelf at greatly reduced prices.

Chapter 7:
Branding, Inquiry Generation

Branding: 70% Market Analysis, Strategy & Planning

Although the concept behind Branding is simple and it makes many business execs feel important to talk about it, effective execution is far from easy. To develop an effective Branding program you must use as much market research as you can, including Analytics gleaned from SEO and Social Media, to determine:

1. What markets and market segments can most benefit from the products and services you offer

2. Identify the top two or three segments, those that account for the bulk of your product's sales

3. Identify the wants and needs of the key prospects, and determine how well you satisfy those wants and needs vs. your competitors. Take the rose-colored glasses off when you do this. Assuming you excel in certain ones, make sure the areas where you are superior are at least as important – if not more so – to your prospects as those where your competitors excel.

4. What concise (25 words or less) and readily understood message best conveys your ability to satisfy the highly important wants and needs where you excel? Creating this message is much easier said than done. Your first try will be good, but not good enough. Keep working on it till it's compelling and powerful.

5. Circulate this message throughout your organization – especially Sales to be sure everyone is on board with it. Painful as it may be, adjust the statement as necessary – but keep it short and compelling.

6. How will you effectively convey that message to prospects? Achieving this is much more complex and costly than it was during the Golden Age of Marketing, before the One-Minute Management Mentality crippled trade-magazine advertising – especially B2B. Now, instead of selecting the magazine(s) that could deliver your top prospects, in most cases marketers now have to search for and procure prospect lists and conduct expensive telemarketing programs. On the other hand Social Media makes this much less expensive and more effective if your offering matches the market segments it delivers well.

7. What available media will you use, including SEO and Social Media? Can you get by with a minimal investment by using just the Internet? Lots of firms think they can and many of them are disappointed. More often than not, you'll want to publicize and promote your offering through niche publications, broadcast media, direct mail or trade shows.

8. None of this is inexpensive, so how much will it cost? Can you afford to do it as often as it takes to make your message register effectively?

9. Can you afford to do it over an extended period of time?

Branding is hard. Branding is costly. Branding is forever. Branding must be a total company commitment to giving customers and prospects everything they expect from a superior, committed organization.

Branding is every public thing you do.

Branding is more than the obvious like ads and publicity, your website, your brochures and newsletters, and the media that carry your message – including Social Media. Branding is every public thing you do – including:

- Product quality and packaging
- Users Manuals (appearance, ease of use, understandability, etc.)
- Your supply chain: Sales/service staff, dealers, distributors, etc.
- Speedy, on-time delivery
- Competent, courteous installation and start-up
- Customer Service in all its forms – with special emphasis on "Prompt Response to Needs and Requests"
- Your website and letterhead
- The letters, themselves, including proper grammar and spelling
- Sales presentations and sales materials
- Your Receptionist and the way you answer the phones
- Your building, location and furniture – including their cleanliness, etc.
- How fast you pay your bills and deal with suppliers
- There's more, but you get the point.

Strong Brands have value

In the 1980s and 90s, building brand awareness (customers and prospects who recognize the name of your company and your products or services) and brand perception (the opinion that customers and prospects have of your company and your products or services) was viewed realistically. It was understood that lots of time, money and effort were required to create these building blocks for a company's success and profitability. Today too many business execs talk about branding as though you can buy it by the pound at your local supermarket.

Because counting clicks, inquiries and downloads is much easier to assess than is company awareness, perception and preference among prospects, clicks and inquiries are accorded much more management attention than are brand awareness and preference. Yet it's brand awareness and preference – plus the efforts of the sales force in presenting the offering and making the close – that bring in the revenues and profits.

Downloads and requests for information are important too. They show who the prospects are, but if a value has to be put on the overall investment, the impact on your company's good name would be at least double that of the much more visible and easier to count clicks and inquiries. So don't make Branding decisions on just those numbers alone. Momentary clicks are the worst measure you can use. They equate to someone reading your ad and taking no further action to learn more information. Counting clicks is similar to the nice warm feeling you get when you learn what percent of the people saw your ad or news release. One consolation though: your brand awareness will likely increase with any added exposure these clicks – or ad readership – will give you. However, you can't be sure whether your brand perception and brand preference has been affected positively or adversely, so don't cheer too loudly.

Branding, Inquiry Generation

Branding is vital. Branding has value. Branding has just one purpose – to help sell your product or service. But don't kid yourself; branding is hard. Branding is something a company must do consistently – week after week, month after month, year after year to get to the top of the pack, and stay there. About 20 years ago, Marketers had a phrase for this: "top of mind awareness." This meant that your brand was one of the first things prospects thought of when they thought of that product or service.

Money well spent

That strong brands have value is demonstrated by one of the world's leading hand-tool manufacturers. Their brand is not only a badge of honor that Construction Pros use to signify their status by wearing it on their belts; the brand also has proven value as well. Several years ago market data showed that one of their lines – despite several low-cost competitors – had a 50 percent unit share. Half of all these types of tools that were bought bore the company's brand. More importantly, the company had a 60 percent revenue share. <u>Their brand commanded a 20 percent premium, on average, over all of the same type of products that were purchased.</u>

<u>Strong customer relationships often trump strong brands:</u>

OK, strong brands have value. But customer-dealer relationships can often be stronger, as a different world-renowned manufacturer with an equally powerful brand discovered. When asked for a price concession from a leading equally respected Home Improvement chain, the world-renowned company declined. The Home Improvement chain took on a lesser-known but top-quality brand for the price they requested. In less than a year the manufacturing giant that had been replaced by the chain belatedly agreed to meet the offer, which they had previously rejected. Instead of having the earlier exclusive, they now share shelf space with that lesser-known brand.

Underestimating the time, money and effort it takes to build a brand – another big mistake.

Several years ago I was VP Marketing for a worldwide, well-respected, well-known company that manufactured digital readouts (DROs). These were used to measure very small units of distance (thousandths of an inch) in high-accuracy manufacturing and measurement situations. Because the name of the company was so well known we had brand recognition that exceeded 80 percent – and benefited by that. The DRO portion of the business was sold, and what had been the brand name of the DRO now became the company name. To the shock and dismay of the new ownership, their name recognition tumbled from 80-plus percent to 18 percent overnight – despite the hundreds of thousands of dollars of advertising and promotion dollars that had been invested to establish the DRO's trade-name brand over the years.

To repeat: It takes years of effort and expense just to build a brand. There are no shortcuts, no easy ways to do this – just time, effort, diligence, and lots of money and patience. There are a very few exceptions where brands became well known in a short period of time – but in those cases millions of dollars were spent to achieve this – or the product was such a break-through that it benefited from scads of national publicity over fairly long periods of time – or the product was used by almost everyone on a day-in, day-out basis. Computers and software are two examples.

Branding: 30% Creative Execution:

AIDA makes your message really sing.

The technique for developing sales messages is as tried and true as the opera AIDA:
- Attention
- Interest
- Desire
- Action

They're the four elements essential to any effective sales message.

1. Attention: Grab the prospects with a strong visual and interesting headline – one that supports and relates to your product or service. This is necessary in virtually every instance except for brochures and websites where prospects have already expressed interest in your company and its offerings.

2. Interest: Intrigue the prospects with a strong, short message that highlights the benefits you offer, and tells how you do it in a way that's better than anybody else. Make sure those benefits meet the top wants & needs of the prospects.

3. Desire: Entice them with added reasons why they should want your offering now, or in the near future. Be factual. Be brief.

4. Action: Ask the prospects to do something positive. Buy it. Try it. Visit your website or your office. Talk to a satisfied customer. Attend a seminar or trade show. Anything – but exhort them to take some action.

Effective presentations and ads can take a variety of forms. Here are some of the more common ones:

1. <u>Case histories:</u> These usually get the best readership and viewership. They are a combination of a highly believable testimony plus a how-to story on how to improve things.

2. <u>Testimonials or Endorsements:</u> Coming from real people these have good credibility and help prove the claims you're making. Coming from celebrities, you're buying the attention the celebrity commands, but it doesn't add a lot to the credibility of the message.

3. <u>Product-Feature-Benefit:</u> These are the most common of all ads and presentations. They highlight the product or service and the claims you want to make. When you use this method, make sure to emphasize the benefits the prospects receive, not just the features you provide. Also, ensure that the benefits you provide are in sync with the prospects' top wants and needs – and that you are superior in those areas.

4. <u>Word Play:</u> Except for billboards these often don't register well, as this example shows: "We've been through the mill." was one headline I wrote as part of a campaign that included four other cutesy headlines. Mercifully, I can only recall two others: "Common Denominator" and "Shock Absorber." Everybody in the agency loved them. In fact, other copywriters would ask me if they could use them as examples of their work when they went on job interviews. (There's no honor in this world.) The client also loved them and they breezed through the approval process. Unfortunately the readers of the magazines in which they appeared didn't share their enthusiasm. Readership was only fair. Gimmicks usually don't work that well.

5. <u>Sound and Visual Effects:</u> Today, with remotes in the viewers' hands, it's all too easy for them to switch channels when ads come on. To attract and hold viewers, advertisers are using unusual sounds and visuals to attract attention. This is a two-edged sword, and just as often is an added irritant, which can alienate them, cause them to turn you off, and worst of all – hurt your image.

Here are some other things that don't work so well:

1. <u>Clownish or silly props:</u> These get attention, which is about all they do. They're bad for your image and don't create interest or desire – numbers 2 & 3 in the key steps for preparing effective sales presentations and advertisements.

2. <u>Blatant sex or innuendo:</u> These also get attention, but most times not in the way you want. They offend many people, unless that's the market you're targeting, and can harm your image.

3. <u>Family members</u>: Ad agencies and media types use this ploy to get you to advertise. It's a strong appeal to your pride, but it rarely appeals to prospects.

4. <u>Brag & Boast:</u> These are ads where the company tells you how great they are – not by emphasizing their benefits and features – but by telling you how smart and inventive they are. These messages should be reserved for capability brochures, which are mentioned in the next section. Even in capability brochures, restrain your emotions and don't break your arm patting yourself on the back.

5. <u>Come-ons:</u> These are ruses where prospects are suckered into reading and acting on a promise of getting great savings on

products that curiously just sold out, for example. Time was, only shady retailers used this scam. Today, thanks to the Internet, they're even more common – and used by many so-called reputable companies. What makes these so self-defeating is the resentment and anger these produce among heretofore trusting prospects.

6. <u>Sound and Visual Effects:</u> This has already been discussed above. Sound and Visual Effects are two-edged swords and should be used with care. Irritating the viewer is not a good Branding technique. Loud volume, which is pervasive in commercials for cars (maybe the dealers and manufacturers spend too much time at NASCAR races), can also be very irritating and likely turns off as many viewers as they attract.

Eschew arcane, sesquipedalian locution

In other words, keep your sales messages clear, simple, direct and persuasive. Don't try to impress prospects with your extensive vocabulary or knowledge of jargon. If your messages must include technical words or phrases because of the markets you serve, that's fine – just so long as your target audience understands it. If you interrupt your prospects' thought processes or send them to the dictionary, you'll invariably lose them.

This is not to say that sales messages should sink to the level of grade-school copy. Find the happy medium. William F. Buckley and James J. Kilpatrick, both outstanding writers and journalists, had a years-long debate over the type of vocabulary that should be used. Buckley maintained that the word that exactly described the thought you wanted to convey – no matter how obscure – was the best word. Kilpatrick maintained that words that confounded the reader weren't the best words to use. In the case of sales messages, there's no denying that Kilpatrick wins the argument.

Ads and other forms of sales messages have just one purpose: to sell or to help sell something. Flaunting your superior vocabulary or esoteric knowledge doesn't make you sound like someone most prospects would like to do business with.

Go with the flow

Good promotional copy should be conversational – not chatty – conversational. The copy should flow: Not too many short, choppy sentences strung together, or too many complex sentences. I don't know how else to say it, but good sales copy will "flow" – make it inviting for the reader to read – all the way to the end, which will include your bid for action. Your bid for action is the whole purpose of the sales message after all.

"Don't take counsel of your fears."

These wise words from General George S. Patton mean: "don't let unknowns dictate your actions." When creating advertising campaigns, especially, don't worry about what the competition is doing before you begin your strategy and planning. It only stifles creativity. There's plenty of time to do that after you've come up with best ideas you can. There's a belief among too many Marketing execs that you should first examine all the competing campaigns to learn what the competition is doing. This often limits creative thinking and kills great ideas before they're born.

The same is true with campaigns designed by committee. As the old saying goes, a camel is a horse designed by a committee.

Promotional materials: print and electronic

Product brochures are supposed to support the sales presentation, as well as be used to respond to inquiries from prospects. When preparing product brochures or websites, there's a strong tendency to envision the prospects relaxing in their chairs and reading your sales message as they would an interesting novel. This is hardly ever the case. The prospects are usually taking time out of their busy work schedule to learn more about the product or system they're evaluating – and your brochure is only one of several that they'll be reading in order to make the best selection for their company.

Brochures should be primarily designed to aid and support the sales effort. The best way to organize a brochure is to first do an outline that simulates a Power Point or flipchart sales presentation. In a sales presentation, the benefit that you provide, which is of greatest importance to the prospect and which you have superiority over competition, should be highlighted on the first slide or page – and the features that support or prove that benefit are summarized, or bulleted beneath.

The second slide or page highlights the next most-important benefit your product or system provides, and the supporting features are discussed below that.. The third slide or page highlights the third most-important benefit you provide, and so on. Follow this outline when preparing the brochure, and review it with salespeople who know the markets and prospects well. In many instances the same important feature that makes your product or system so valuable to the prospects will need to be mentioned under two or more of the benefits. Don't be reluctant to do this, but phrase things differently to keep readers interested.

Another important thing to remember is that in most cases the brochures are used for and during sales presentations, and not primarily to answer inquiries that come by email or snail mail. The salesperson is usually sitting across the desk or table from the prospects with the brochure positioned so it's clearly readable by them. Hence, it's upside-down to the salesperson, and is difficult to read at best. (Speaking of difficulty reading, computers are commonly used instead of brochures. Prospects often can't see the information clearly, even if they don't say so, when asked.)

Whether using brochures or computers, the key sales points (benefits and major features) should be made prominent. This not only makes for better presentations, it also makes reading more inviting and effective when the prospect is reviewing things later.

Capability brochures are used in addition to product brochures when a company wants to impress prospects with the expertise of its personnel, and the extent and quality of the company's investment in their tools for production and quality assurance. While both the product and capability stories can be told in one brochure, when a company has two or more separate products in its line, it's often less expensive to produce a separate brochure that can be used with any of the products. For service providers the capability brochure is usually the basic sales aid.

Capability brochures should be prepared in the same manner as product brochures with the most-persuasive customer-prospect benefit stated on the front cover or first page, followed by the supporting features. The second most-important benefit comes next, and so on.

Websites & CDs: Websites give you the best of both worlds. They are, or can be both a video and a brochure all in one. But these very strengths present a real danger. They give the creator of the site so much latitude of design that there's a tendency for many designers to make the site too gimmicky. So gimmicky that it gets in the way of the basic purpose of the site.

To give an example, I visited the site of a winery with one simple objective: I wanted to buy a bottle of wine. When I got to the site, I was presented with a beautiful, panoramic view of the vineyard – but I couldn't figure out how to place an order. On further inspection of this beautiful vista, I noticed one moving object – a rocking chair near the top of the screen. I clicked on the rocking chair – and Voila!! Another screen popped up and said: "Let's sit down a talk a while."

I didn't want to sit and talk; I wanted to buy a bottle of wine.

The message: Don't let your messages get in the way of a sale. Give the customers what they want: A fast, easy way to buy your product, if that's what they want to do. This is not to say you shouldn't feature sales information about your product or service. By all means, do so. Follow the same method of organization that has proved to work so well with brochures. But give the prospects a ready, easy way to buy, if that's what they want to do.

Another caveat about videos and CDs: Just because you've spent a lot of time, money and creativity to prepare a CD, don't assume the prospects are going to pop it into their computers – as simple and easy as it is. I learned this the hard way. We produced a CD that was really great. It not only showed the product in operation, it also let the prospects demo the product themselves. It really put them behind the wheel and let them test-drive it. It cost us a lot of time and money to produce it.

We mailed it out to prospects, and when we called to follow up to be sure they had received it, a high percentage told us that they had, but they hadn't yet viewed it. They told us they had it on their desks and would view it that day. When we followed up a couple of days later, we got the same story. Then the same story again – and again.

Just because you've created a great CD, don't expect the world to beat a path to your door. Going back to the AIDA principle, we had definitely gotten the attention of our prospects, but we hadn't aroused their interest sufficiently – the second stage in the process for developing sales presentations.

Trying to sell by phone or the Internet, while relatively inexpensive is not very effective, as many marketers will tell you. I have found that sending emails and following them up by phone greatly increases the likelihood of response by the prospects. Not with our CD, however. In the case of our CD, we had two options we could have taken:

1. Hire sales reps who would work on a straight commission
2. Conduct a high-impact direct-mail campaign to select prospects

We did neither, which was a mistake. We should have done the latter, based on our budget constraints.

<u>High-impact, high-response mailing programs:</u> If you're introducing a new product, a major improvement or just want to emphasize some special capabilities your company has, consider a high-impact direct-mail program that consists of board games or inexpensive trinkets that people can keep, or give to their kids. Tie them into the service or product you offer by using "borrowed interest" or some interesting theme or headline that relates to the message you want to convey, and do more than one mailing.

This concept is based on three principles:

1. Everybody likes pleasant surprises

2. Everybody likes to get gifts

3. Everybody likes a laugh

Programs like these can be relatively inexpensive when used with select groups to powerfully register a few important messages. When I was with a manufacturer of Scientific Instruments, which were sold nationwide, through two national distributors, we used a yearlong monthly program that was sent to 1,200 distributor salespeople to:

a) Remind them about our line

b) Enthuse them about our line

c) Remind them of key sales points about our several products

In just three months the distributor salespeople, who hadn't been that interested in our line before, were asking our salespeople, "Hey, what's next month's surprise going to be?" The program also caught the attention of their Senior Management who also started to talk up our line.

The result: Sales rose – and continued to rise.

I've done similar programs with board games like Monopoly:

a) using Monopoly money to tell a profitability story

b) using the tokens to make a point using borrowed interest

c) using deeds to property to make similar points

In each of these we asked the prospects to read a brief message and answer two or three simple, obvious questions about the message. This helped reinforce the key sales points we wanted to emphasize. Anyone who responded to even one mailing got a complete board game with a recap of our features and benefits.

What's more, our relationships and recognition among our prospect base improved markedly.

Think like the customer.

To learn how to master the art and science of creating persuasive sales materials – or teach someone in your organization to do it – start with sales letters. Sales letters include, or should include, all the key elements that should be in other types of sales material. A good sales letter will be concise – no more than two pages, including the inside address, the salutation and the sign-off. One page is even better. If more information is required, include a brochure or mailer, but keep your letter short if you want it to be read. Between the inside address and the salutation you might want to add a pithy one-line bold-faced statement that identifies the subject you're talking about. This is your headline, so to speak.

The first paragraph of the letter should get right to the point – including your value proposition. The next two or three paragraphs should give the prospect more reasons to buy or to consider what you're trying to sell. The closing paragraph should include a promise to follow up on your letter in a few days. Be absolutely sure this happens – even if it's just to ask if the letter was received and read.

Whether it's a sales letter or any other type of promotional material, once it's written, lean back in your chair and put yourself in the shoes of the customers and prospects. Review what's been written through their eyes – not yours. Will the readers understand what you're trying to say? Will they be interested or motivated by your selling proposition? Think very hard about this before you make it public.

If it ain't broke, don't fix it.

This sin is so common it's almost universal – especially on the B2B side. Even for a seasoned professional, it's difficult to know when a good promotional program has run its course. In the consumer market advertisers have access to more and better readership data than when selling B2B, but even then it's not easy to assess accurately.

In B2B your best – and virtually only – source is the number and quality of inquiries you get as a result of your promotional campaign.

The Sales Force can often give you input on this, but balance their input with the real activity you're getting from your ad campaign and website.

Why Acu-Rite didn't go "On & On"

When I was Sales Manager for that manufacturer of scientific instruments, I also wore the Marketing Communications Manager's hat. We had been running a highly effective, well-read, case-history ad campaign for over two years. The campaign also featured a prominent and memorable slogan: "Acu-Rite Goes On & On." The slogan had become so popular and well received we also produced a song for it, "The On & On" hustle.

(This was during the disco days.) When we converted to a new campaign, we dropped the slogan.

Three or four months later, I was at a major trade show and walked over to a booth where a prospect was exhibiting his products. I introduced myself and had no more than mentioned my company name than the prospect grinned broadly, pointed at me, and exclaimed: "Acu-Rite Goes On & On."

I was delighted that he knew and liked the slogan, but I was really chagrined that the Ad Agency and Ad Manager (me) had dropped such a great slogan and ad campaign so soon. Ad Agencies and Ad Managers usually get tired of their great promotional programs long before customers and prospects do, which is why many of today's advertisers change their slogans almost as often as they change their socks.

The moral: If it ain't broke, don't fix it.

CHAPTER 8:
PROSPECT IDENTIFICATION AND DEVELOPMENT

While I've referred favorably to the Golden Age of Marketing-Sales before, it still had its problems: Prospect Identification and Development has always been – and continues to be – a problem area that only a small fraction of companies deal with successfully. Today, there's heavy emphasis on clicks and downloads via the Internet. Yesterday, it was inquiries in the form of requests for more information on a company's products and services as a result of its promotional efforts via the printed and spoken word. Chapters 6 and 7 discussed the many activities required for effective Branding and Inquiry Generation among your prospects. Neither is easy, and both require much time, talent, money and dedication to do them effectively and efficiently. Branding is hard. Branding is costly. Branding is forever. So is Prospect Identification and Development – and if history is any bench-mark it's much harder, and it's not handled as well by most companies. There are reasons for this:

a) Marketing Communications believes every inquiry they get is golden and should get prompt follow up by Sales.

b) Social Media practitioners believe their clicks and downloads are just as important – or even more so because of the immediacy of the Internet.

c) Both departments rely on complicated esoteric formulas for Analytics to verify them and are sure that their inquiries have value and believe they should be acted upon before the competition can get into the act.

The truth is: none of this is true, and today's belief that all clicks have lots of value is a pipe dream. Clicks of less than ten seconds have the same value as someone glancing at your ad, but lacking an interest, so they don't take further action. Just as the viewing of the ad may have increased brand awareness, so do momentary clicks help increase brand awareness, but the value ends there.

<u>Case History #1:</u> Back during the Golden Age of Marketing-Sales the media – B2B magazines especially – promoted the myth that all inquiries (inquiries from prospects who had a sufficient interest in a company's products or services that they requested more information) would result in a sale. As the myth went, one of the three inquiries would be a sale for your product, no matter what you did. Another would result in a sale for the competition, no matter what you or they did. The third inquiry (no one could predict which) was the one you could win by taking prompt, effective sales action.

<u>Case History #2:</u> I had a friend who started an Inquiry Follow-up and Qualification service in the mid 1980s. He'd call people who inquired about his clients' products or services to be certain they had a genuine interest and intent to make a purchase for their or a competitor's offering. He made up to seven calls per inquirer to ascertain their intent. Despite all these calls, only ten percent of those who inquired about the products or services confirmed that they had an intention to buy some company's offerings. Over the years that percentage dwindled to six percent because the quality of the prospects degraded for various reasons. Needless to say, he abandoned the business.

Case History #3: Several years ago a survey was conducted among people who had asked for information about products or services. It demonstrated that companies are far more eager to sell their products than prospects are to buy:

a) Only 40 percent of prospects who had requested information on the offering made purchases within six months of requesting and receiving information.

b) 30 percent made purchases between six months and a year after receiving the information requested.

c) The other 30 percent didn't make a purchase until a year or more after they had received the information requested.

If you doubt these results, just think about how many months you spent evaluating the last major purchase you made. All this may help explain why the percentage of people who request information and are genuine prospects appears to be so low.

Prospect Identification and Qualification remain one of the most stubbornly unsolvable mysteries in Marketing-Sales. In the old days before the Internet, the main barrier to contacting the prospect was known as "the dragon at the gate," the person who protected the presumed prospect, who inquired about your product or service, from having to talk with you. I use the word presumed because people have many reasons for making inquiries:

- They may be planning a purchase sometime in the future, and are collecting information for further evaluation with a sincere intention to buy
- They may have already determined the brand they intend to buy and are building a case for that decision
- They may just want that information for their files

Whatever their reasons, most of them are not ready or willing to talk with a salesperson any time soon. On the other hand, they may be, and that's why following up on requests for information is so essential. I personally know of some Sales Managers who believe that all inquiries should be followed up on. They maintain – and rightly so – that it's important to establish relationships with all likely prospects, whether a sale results or not. This makes good sense since the majority of sales don't occur until six months after a request for information is made.

When I was Publisher of some Manufacturing Management magazines we had many hundreds of advertisers, and only two – two count 'em two – conducted serious prospect identification and qualification programs on a long-term basis. Both were outside the US – in fact, both were Israeli.

Today, there are many purveyors of software programs who claim to be able to identify these prospects for you. While I haven't reviewed them all, I haven't found any that can really do the job. No matter how many contacts or how many teasers they're sent, if the prospects don't want to talk with you, they won't. Also, it takes a serious commitment on the part of top management to adopt and finance a long-term prospect identification and qualification program. Many have tried and most have thrown in the towel much too soon because they lacked the will to see the fruits of their promotional programs through to the finish.

My friend who established that identification and qualification service, which proved itself to work, failed to keep clients for much more than a year – mainly because client management lost the will to see their investment through to the end. It was easier to give the leads to the sales force and let them toss the prospects they don't know into the round file so they could concentrate on the prospects they do know.

Top management needs to think seriously about this: What good are all your company's promotional efforts if you're not willing to make the final effort to capitalize on your investments?

My recommendation: Turn your inquiries over to specific persons in Customer Service who are tasked to follow up on all inquiries, or assign the task to Sales Trainees. It's a great way for them to learn the frustrations of selling – and the patience and persistence it requires. Do not assign the task to someone in Marketing Communications or the Social Media operation to do it. They'll have a strong inclination to gild the lily. After all, inquiries are what they're all about, and it's to their advantage to have as high a positive response rate as possible. Again, do not use an outside service that isn't fully committed to the inquiry-qualification process and is proven to be reputable – for obvious reasons.

Two more words of advice:
- Know when enough is enough. Today, many people hide behind their voice-mail messaging and don't answer messages. If they persist in ignoring you, they're likely not interested – or at least not interested at this time.
- Have a workable contact strategy in effect. One that has proven to be effective is to first call them, identify yourself on the voice mail, and tell the prospect you'll follow up with an e-mail or letter. Send your message promptly and if they don't respond, follow up with another phone call.

If neither of these gets a response, have a program where you follow up on a monthly or periodic basis with a newsletter or e-message that's truly relevant to their interest and invites response. You can also learn a lot about these prospects by visiting their websites or using other types of Analytics.

Chapter 9:
Why the Marketing-Sales Team Isn't really a Team

Prospect qualification and development, which was just discussed, has been the giant donut hole in Marketing-Sales for decades. Historically, Marketing Communications generated inquiries from prospects, and then gave them to Sales for follow up. Except for trade shows, where Sales is usually directly involved, when they get inquiries from Marketing Communications they typically thumb through them and:

a) Put people and companies they recognize in the follow-up file

b) Put people and companies they don't recognize in the round file

Funny isn't it? MarComm/Social Media is supposed to generate inquiries from people and companies that are not known to be prospects, but might be. Yet that's exactly what Sales is throwing away. (I saw this happen more than once when I was National Sales Manager.) Analytics can be a valuable aid in this if the Analytics can clearly identify a strong prospect, who should be avidly courted and developed.

But Sales isn't the real culprit in all of this. Salespeople already have too much non-selling work to do. As it is, they only get to spend about 30 percent of their time in front of customers and prospects, and only about half of that actually selling, what with using much valuable time in front of the buyer to re-establish rapport, answer questions or discuss the news of the day, etc. etc.

As we've discussed, the culprit is the system that's not in place – a coordinated Prospect Qualification & Development system – and hundreds of business execs agree. 722 US business execs responded to a survey thusly:

1. Almost 60 percent said their companies only convert 10 percent of their leads to sales
2. Another 60 percent said company revenues could be increased 15 percent or more with proper follow up
3. 53 percent said their company had no formal process for qualifying and validating new-business opportunities
4. Only half of the execs thought Marketing-Sales worked well together on projects that required teamwork
5. A paltry 7 percent said Marketing-Sales teamed effectively on new-business development

To repeat: If senior management really believes this and wants to reap more of its substantial investment in advertising, publicity, trade shows; newsletters, direct mailing; websites, social media, and other promotional efforts – it will institute an Inquiry Qualification & Development system using Customer Service or Sales Trainees to do it.

Sales & Marketing: Taking separate paths to reach the same goal:

While that survey of 722 US business execs, just mentioned, is eye opening – and in some cases shocking – it's really not too surprising when you think about it. Salespeople and Marketing Communications people are very different animals that see things very differently as well:

1. Salespeople see the trees, not the forest. They are on the firing line every day, seeing real-world customers react to their

company's products in the form of compliments, questions, or complaints

2. Marketing/Social Media people see the forest, not the trees. They are sure in their beliefs about the markets, products and prospects. They are sure their ads, sales materials and websites are fine just as they are. After all, management approved them, didn't they?

Being on the firing line every day, salespeople receive information that makes up bits and pieces of the whole picture. It's only bits and pieces, but it's often valuable information, both as to the company's products and those of the competitors. Sometimes the information is obvious, such as the spectrophotometer with the built-in computer that operated independently. Sometimes it isn't.

Since salespeople have a real-world understanding of the individual prospect's opinions and preferences, Top Management and the Marketing-Sales group should gather input from them more than once a year in sales meetings. More frequent interaction is needed – let's say joint calls on a quarterly basis – especially by top management and Marketing Communications.

Doublespeak

George Orwell's "Animal Farm" refers to "Doublespeak" as what Big Brother would tell the people to sugarcoat the truth. It's used here to illustrate the variance between what the sales force tells prospects and what the company wants to communicate to the marketplace. It's not that either party is trying to mislead anyone; it's just that they speak different languages.

When I was an Account Exec with Ad Agencies, I'd interview salespeople to learn the key features and benefits they emphasized when talking with customers and prospects. I often heard things that didn't correspond to what management believed were their company's strongest sales points. It's not that Marketing-Sales aren't on the same team. They're just not on the same page. Oral communication is often different from the printed word.

Since Sales and Marketing Communications often don't speak the same language, management must take pains to ensure the key messages dovetail. This is not to say the salespeople should use canned sales pitches. It's just that they should have the Value Proposition and key sales points down pat.

"Don't just stand there. Do something."

Reflecting back on that survey of 722 business execs, think about the disconnection – not just between Sales & MarComm, but also between Sales, MarComm, and the rest of the organization. If a condition existed where manufacturing costs were out of whack, you can bet your life that Manufacturing and Engineering would surely meet to try to solve the problem. If they didn't do it of their own accord, the CEO would make sure they did – and fast. But this rarely happens between Sales and Marketing Communications – yet they both report to the same boss. Also, meetings with Sales are rarely scheduled with other departments in the company – even during the annual sales meetings, which is truly a lost opportunity.

As the survey shows, this disconnect often goes untreated, and is usually allowed to persist by management at all levels. I can't prove this, but I do know that when I was Marketing Communications Manager for the Fortune-100 company that manufactured Scientific Instruments, I used to joke that my department operated like an independent satellite – I rarely got questioned on our activities. It's not that Management didn't care; it's just that they didn't quite understand how we did what we did. They just knew that we did it – and nobody was complaining so that was enough to satisfy them.

Left hand vs. right hand

The main reason why the gulf between Marketing-Sales persists to this day is that neither side understands what motivates the other. As I mentioned before, MarComm/Social Media is driven by Inquiries, Clicks, Downloads, etc. because that's what management measures, so that's what they get. In Chapter two, I mentioned that one of the crippling diseases is "Management by use of visible figures only." When it comes to inquiries, they're all that are plainly visible so that's what gets the attention.

As National Sales Manager, I was given the added job of Marketing Communications Manager, because I knew the function well. When I'd make calls on our Industrial Distributors, I'd ask them what we could do to help them increase sales. They'd invariably reply, "Advertise for me. Give me leads." On follow-up calls I'd ask them about the leads we were supplying them. They'd invariably reply, "Oh, they were all junk; we just threw them away."

Okay, some of them may not have been true prospects, but some of them had to have value. Despite these frustrations, I learned a lot about the wants and needs of the distributors and their customers during these calls, so every call we made helped me understand the markets better. I tell these stories to better explain why the information gap between Marketing-Sales exists, and why it exists. The Sales department doesn't sufficiently understand MarComm/Social Media and how it can help them, and MarComm/Social Media doesn't sufficiently understand Sales and how they can be helped. The solution: the two functions must spend more time working with each other, learning to respect each other, and understand each other. Plus, the CMO must truly understand both operations and must assure that the managers of each function have mutual respect for each other, and understand and support each other.

"Old Glory"

To illustrate this phenomenon a bit more: my boss, the President of the Division, liked to tell this story: He was trying to get funding for a new flagpole in front of the building – the cost was less than $3,000. He was in front of the corporate Operating Committee to defend this modest request <u>for the third time.</u> With a mixture of humor and exasperation he said: "My Marketing Communications Manager spends 50 times that much money every month, and no one ever asks him any questions!!"

With a little bit of counter-humor himself, the CEO replied "Maybe we should get him up here too."

Don't get me wrong: I had to present and defend my business plan every year, and include detailed budgets and rationales each time. It was reviewed and approved by top corporate management as well. But once I got that OK, I was on my own – regardless of how well my department's efforts helped increase sales or supported the Sales Force's efforts. It wasn't until I managed both operations simultaneously – and understood how one could improve the other's effectiveness – that the two functions truly meshed and became a process.

"You can't lead from behind."

General James Longstreet – in my opinion the greatest battlefield commander in the Civil War – once told General Lee, who asked him to be careful of his safety when leading his troops into battle: "You can't lead from behind, sir." If company management really wants to know what customers and prospects want and need, they should follow that advice and travel with the sales force quarterly – plus spend a few days (not just a few hours) at major trade shows meeting and talking with customers and prospects.

Also, Sales should be included in the process of developing the all-important positioning statement or value proposition for the company. Since Marketing has a better understanding of the overall market, the company's relative strengths and weaknesses, and its strategies, they should balance their perceptions with that of the sales force – which they all too often don't.

This dichotomy between Sales & Marketing Communications frequently manifests itself when it comes to trade show exhibits. Marketing Communications wants the overall theme and appearance of the exhibit to be an extension of the national marketing campaigns. This is both reasonable and makes good business sense. Plus, the budget for exhibits usually falls under that department, so the exhibit is "theirs," so to speak.

The sales force, on the other hand, has to man the booth and take valuable selling time away from their territories to do their share for the company. This costs them in lost commissions and lost selling time in their territories, so they have a justifiable claim to make on the appearance of the booth and its content. They want a booth that helps them demo and sell products.

Since I have been on both sides of the fence during my checkered career, I know that this is fact – not theory. Another fact is that inquiries need to be qualified and developed in a different and better way than they are currently handled in most organizations. While the previous chapter discussed this at some length, this cannot be said enough:

Inquirers Take the Path of Least Resistance

Of the several gulfs that separate MarComm/Social Media from Sales, the Sea of Clicks & Inquiries is one of the largest. MarComm/Social Media thinks all inquiries are golden. Salespeople are sure most of them are dross.

Most often, clicks and inquiries are the be-all and the end-all of all promotional efforts. They're proof that real, live people expressed interest in the company's offering. Presidents and CEOs are one of the main causes of this fixation on the importance of clicks and inquiries. They're a quick n'easy way to judge the value of the promotional programs. It's not that way in the real world, however.

Not all inquirers are good prospects: The evaluation process that prospects go through takes time – it's not immediate by any means, except in a few instances. Also, many inquirers are collecting information on the products or services that are available so that they can make comparisons to clarify or justify offerings that they already have decided upon. Another thing: lots fewer of them are hot prospects. Research shows that only forty percent of purchases are made within six months of requesting the information. If you doubt those findings, think about the time you spend evaluating cars before you make a purchase.

When you conduct a prospect-development program the quality of your customer and prospect list is very important. Have the sales force build a complete list of all customers – both old and new. By old, go back to sales that were made a few years ago and include all companies that bought from you and where Sales thinks contact still has business value. Make sure the contact info they give you is current, and that it's kept current going forward. Do the same with prospects.

The ABCs of Prospecting

Going back as far as I can remember, prospects have been categorized according to their sales potential – both as to the amount they could purchase and to the likelihood of their doing business with you. In chapter five we used the hand-tool market to illustrate this point:

- The Contractor Pros, who were just about 5 percent of the more than 90 million people who bought hand tools each year, accounted for about half of all dollar purchases, so they were undoubtedly "A" prospects.
- Moderate and Serious DIYers are more or less in the middle so they're mostly "B" prospects.
- Light DIYers, who make up 70 percent of the market but only account for about 20 percent of the dollar purchases, would be "C" prospects.

In your prospect-development program you're obviously going to spend more money and effort on the As, less on the Bs, and even less on the Cs. Because there are so many C prospects in most areas of business, it's tough to know where to draw the line to keep your list manageable.

It's not easy to keep the list as long as it needs to be to do a thorough job, but short enough so that you're not wasting promotional dollars on prospects that aren't really good prospects. Just as everybody loves to have a party and nobody wants to clean up afterwards, salespeople are more than happy to develop the list, but when you ask them to delete people who are no longer good prospects it's like pulling teeth. This is the weakness of automated computer-managed programs: You still need the cooperation of the sales force to keep the list both clean and effective, and this chore is more boring to them than doing expense accounts – so good luck.

Prospects are seldom as eager to buy, as you are to sell

As eager as you are to sell your products, few prospects share that enthusiasm. A significant period of time usually elapses between a prospect's request for product information, and when that purchase takes place, as was explained in the previous chapter. In the introduction under "Mismanagement by Objective" I mentioned how – as Marketing Communications Manager – I'd try to increase the number of leads my department would generate every year. I also mentioned how the number of leads from magazine advertising appeared to drop because prospects who wanted more information as a result of seeing that ad or reading that news story went directly to that company's website instead of using the Reader Service cards provided in the magazine.

To offset that downturn in inquiries from Reader Service cards – the primary and virtually only tool that was used to measure the effectiveness of advertising and publicity in any given magazine – magazines resorted to gimmicks that would hype the number of inquiries they generated. The bulk of these added inquiries weren't from genuine prospects – one of the two major reasons for this decline. The second reason is the myth that clicks are an all-important measure of prospect interest. As mentioned before, momentary clicks are no more valid an indicator of a respondent's interest than is measurement of readers who glance at, or skim your ad. In fact, a click could often be nothing more than a mistake.

Sales and MarComm/Social Media are not enemies. They just aren't on the same page. They need more exposure to each other – at headquarters and in the field. It's the job of senior management to make sure this happens.

Chapter 10:
Sales: The Least Time-effective Process in all of Business

The bad news: There's nothing you can do about it. Making the sales process more time-effective is not easy because salespeople have so many unavoidable duties they must perform:

- Call reports
- Expense reports
- Drive/Travel time
- Waiting in the customer's or prospect's office
- Establishing or re-establishing rapport
- Questions and Answers
- Handling complaints
- Reassuring the customers or prospects
- Maintaining relationships

The list goes on. . .

The good news: "The Science of Selling" helps optimize your scarcest asset: Selling time. The many non-selling duties that confront salespeople leave just 30% of their time for them to devote to their primary function: Representing their company's products and services to customers and prospects. Hence it's highly important that this time be used to best advantage.

"The Science of Selling," described in this chapter, explains three essentials salespeople should know in order to maximize their sales effectiveness:

A) How to know and better manage themselves when dealing with others

B) How to recognize their prospects' Social Styles, and adjust to them

C) How to best learn the wants and needs of their prospects

How to better know, and manage yourself:

To know, and to know how to manage your responses and behavior – as well as to better anticipate the behavior of prospects in most selling situations – are highly important for any salesperson. The well-known and highly respected "Myers-Briggs" testing process is an excellent way to learn this. Just Google or Bing "Myers-Briggs" on your computer and answer the several questions they ask. It's easy to do and it's confidential.

Once you've answered the questions, and studied the results, you'll get a better understanding of your Social Style – as well as a detailed description of it. In all, Myers-Briggs identifies and describes 16 different Social Styles, which you can print out for more study and future reference. It's important to note that no one Social Style is superior to any other, nor do the different Social Styles necessarily make anyone any better at a particular trade or profession, or limit a person's management potential. For example, the Myers-Briggs test tells you whether you tend to be:

a. An introvert or an extrovert, and to what degree. (If you're highly introverted, Sales may not be a good career for you.)

b. Whether you are "Sensing" (take things at face value) or are "Intuitive" (interpretive of situations). Intuitiveness is an asset for a good salesperson, but seeing things as they are is important too.

c. Whether you are "Thinking" (judge things based mainly on facts) or "Feeling" (evaluate things from a more personal perspective). Again, a mix of both is good, but pay attention to the rating you get for each. If you're ranked high on one, that's your dominant characteristic.

d. Whether you are "Judging" (decide things quickly) or "Perceiving" (want more information before deciding). Again, pay attention to the spreads. If you're high on the Judging side, you'll need to exercise patience and understanding when trying to sell a Perceiver.

e. How "Flexible" you are. A high level of Inflexibility in a salesperson is a drawback. If you're highly inflexible, you won't be able to negotiate well, or "roll with the punch." If you're overly flexible you'll tend to "give away the store." Everything in moderation, as the Greeks used to say.

Every person is a mixture of these characteristics, but each person possesses them to different degrees and intensities. By studying your own analysis, as well as the other information provided by the Myers-Briggs site, you can prepare yourself to better judge how your prospects are likely to react to various selling situations, and estimate how best to prepare both yourself and your sales presentation.

Other capabilities that you can also practice and develop include:

1. Adjusting your style to better relate to people with Social Styles that are different from yours. That's a form of Flexibility.

2. Learning how to really listen.

3. Knowing when to stop talking, and start asking questions.

4. Knowing how to react and respond to challenges and complaints.

Attributes of good salespeople:

There are almost as many descriptions of "the Sales type" as there are people describing them, but I have found these characteristics to be essential in any successful salesperson:

1. Empathy: Be able to put yourself in the prospects' shoes – think like they do.

2. Strong ego: Not a big ego, a strong one. When your proposals are rejected – which they will be on many occasions – you don't take it personally; just smile and move on to the next prospect.

3. Persistence: Selling takes time and most often, more than one call before you make the sale. You have to keep coming back, again & again. Don't quit too easily or readily, but know when to stop.

4. Self-discipline: This is what gets you up every morning to face a fresh, new world that's just waiting for you to sell them your products. Don't roll over for one more, short snooze.

5. Attentive & Observant: This is another way to say: Be a good listener. Take good notes, and follow up on questions and promises.

6. Inquisitiveness: Not nosy, but intellectually curious. This is particularly important if a salesperson is to master the art of Consultative Selling (see below), which is becoming more important as products and services become more complex.

7. Honesty: In the next Chapter we talk about earning the "Respect & Trust" of your prospects. Most people can smell a phony a mile away. If you're not honest, you won't be a really good salesperson. You may get away with it for a while, but things will eventually catch up with you.

8. Resilience & Flexibility: This is a close cousin to Persistence. It's the elasticity in you that lets you keep bouncing back and knowing when to bend – but not too far. Your degree of Flexibility can also be measured by Myers-Briggs. This is a highly important quality in a salesperson. If you're quite inflexible, you won't be able to negotiate well and should probably find some other line of work. If you're too flexible, you'll probably tend to give away the store. So make sure you measure this and try to master this.

9. Reticence & Tolerance: Also close cousins to Resilience & Flexibility. It's knowing when and how to hold your tongue, and allow room for other points of view.

10. Determination: This is another close relation of Persistence. It's also what keeps you coming back – and back again – but know when to stop wasting your and the prospect's time.

Social Styles: Lessons Long Remembered

Most training sessions that are held at annual sales meetings usually have a shelf life of two weeks to a month. Not with the training on how to analyze and utilize the various Social Styles of customers and prospects, however. Even two years after we held a two-day session on learning our Social Styles, as well as recognizing the Social Styles of others, I had salespeople telling me how they successfully handled a problem situation by stepping back and analyzing why they weren't getting through to the prospect because of the difference in their Social Styles. Even though you can't analyze the Social Styles of your customers and prospects exactly, you can pretty well judge the general category they fall into if you study the sixteen styles outlined in the Myers-Briggs process.

Focus your time and effort where it counts

Seven Sigma Selling: Here are seven tips, based on actual experience that can help salespeople maximize their scarce, but valuable time. They show how to best capitalize on the major wants & needs of top prospects and use selling time most effectively.

1. <u>Prioritize your prospects.</u> Focus your efforts where it really counts. Every market has A, B and C prospects. Avoid the tendency to over-estimate the potential of your prospects. The more of them you incorrectly prioritize the more time and effort you'll spend on them.

Here's a classic example: When I was a magazine publisher there was an advertiser who spent millions of dollars each year on their Consumer business and hundreds of thousands on the B2B side. As one of the poor relations among the many B2B segments they were developing, we eagerly classified them as an A prospect, based solely on budget size and spent much time and treasure pursuing them.

There was just one problem. Because the consumer business was so dominant, they had a consumer ad agency that knew or cared very little about the B2B side, and to keep things simple for the agency the Ad Manager told them to use Association magazines whenever possible. Even though we had more and better prospects than the Association magazine that served our market – as well as better readership – we didn't have a chance to get the business. We banged our heads against this wall for several years before we woke up and realized we were wasting our valuable selling time on a losing proposition.

The moral: Prioritize your prospects: Focus your effort where it counts.

2. Forget your ego: focus on the heavy-user groups. A large well-known precision-tool manufacturer wanted to enter the US Hardware market – over 90 million purchasers a year. It was clear that it would take years of effort to establish adequate brand awareness and market coverage. Further study showed that about five percent of that total – the Contractor Pros – accounted for over fifty percent of the dollar sales. Focusing on them was obviously a very sound and smart sales objective.

It was also known that the Contractor Pros did most of their shopping at Contractor Supply Houses where the manufacturer was already well established and had excellent relationships. Despite all this, most of the salespeople spent most of their selling time trying to sell to Home Improvement Centers – the Big Boxes. Why? Making a sale to the Big Boxes was considered a major sales coup – even though it resulted in fewer commissions for the salespeople in the process.

The moral: Forget your ego. Go where your sales opportunities are greatest and the chances to make the sale are best.

3. Include all major buying influences – learn their major wants and needs. A leading supplier of Scientific Instruments sold through two national distributors and targeted three major markets. Sales had stagnated and began to slump. It was finally recognized that the distributors were just as important to sales as the major end users. Once the distributors began to be treated both as prospects and as partners in selling, and programs were put in place to motivate them, sales rose – and continued to rise.

The moral: Be sure you're targeting all key buying/selling influences.

4. <u>Consider related markets where you can compete</u> – and win. A local magazine targeted Commercial Building Owners and Managers to promote rental space to prospective business tenants. It had strong ad support from the building owners, but sales had peaked. By also touting the readership of businesspeople who were considering relocation, the magazine was able to appeal to several other types of businesses for their advertising as well – new and used office furniture & equipment, interior decorators, computer networking services, suppliers of paint and carpeting, etc.

The moral: Consider related markets where you can compete.

5. <u>Sell the big benefit – not your big feature.</u> An area in which you have a minor advantage over competition, but it is very important to your prospects, will most-often create more sales than an area in which you have a major competitive advantage, but it is of less importance to your prospects.

The moral: Sell the big benefit, not your big feature.

6. <u>Strong customer relationships often trump strong brands.</u> A manufacturer of small, relatively inexpensive machine tools had a large and loyal customer and distributor base across the US. The company was sold to an investment-banking firm that knew very little about the business – and even less about distributors and the important part they played. They wanted to improve the company's profitability, so they decided that they didn't need to "give" the distributors the 15 percent discount they had been earning by selling and servicing the company's equipment. They eliminated the distributors, and in less than a year lost about half their business to competitors they created.

The dumped distributors banded together and bought and branded a close overseas cousin to the once-famous brand. The distributors took the market by storm, using the goodwill they had established with the same customers they had loyally served over the years.

The moral: Strong customer relationships often trump strong brands.

7. <u>Prompt Response to Needs and Requests</u> is second only to low price among most customers and prospects. An organization asked a magazine to conduct a survey among its readers, who were customers and prospects of that organization's members. The organization's members wanted to learn what services – aside from product attributes such as accuracy, reliability, etc. – were most valued. Fourteen of these services were listed.

To almost everyone's surprise, "Prompt Response to Needs and Requests" ranked a very close second to "Low Price." What was ranked third didn't even come close. Prompt response to Needs and Requests costs very little to provide, and you don't have to be a rocket scientist to do it.

The moral: Prompt response to needs and requests is a great sales tool, and a great way to earn respect and trust.

Consultative Selling – Everything Old Is New Again

Consultative Selling has recently become a hot, new topic. But it's easily a half-century old – at least as far as Ad Agencies are concerned. One of the key positions in every Ad Agency was and is the Account Executive who serves the clients, learns their wants and needs – including the wants and needs of their prospects – and distills those wants and needs into language and directions that Ad Copywriters, Art Directors, Artists, Photographers, and Production

Pros can readily understand, so that they can use this knowledge to create strong, persuasive ads, websites, publicity, social media, direct mail programs, sales materials, as well as other recommendations for related promotional activities such as trade shows, seminars and public-speaking engagements.

This is known as "Campaign Planning" and the Account Execs (A/Es) were and are the precursors for what is today called "Consultative Selling" (C/S). Here's how it works: The A/E or C/S visits the client, and during the rapport-building stage of the introductory conversation describes his company's capabilities, experience and client base. The A/E or C/S then learns the basics of the prospective client's business, as well as the wants and needs of customers and prospects by asking several key questions:

1. What are the products or services they provide and want to develop or promote?

2. What do these products or services do? (Applications)

3. Who are their customers or prospects and are there others they wish to serve?

4. What are the key wants and needs of their customers and prospects?

5. What are the features and benefits they provide to these customers and prospects?

6. Who are the competitors?

7. What are the client's strengths and weaknesses relative to the competition?

8. Has the client developed an effective Value Proposition and/or Mission Statement?

9. If not, or if the statements can be improved, chapters five, six, and seven show in detail how to use Social Media and SEO to mine and generate the Analytics that will help optimize the Value Proposition, Elevator Pitch, sales messages and other marketing-sales efforts that help increase revenues and profits, as well as develop ideas for new products or product improvements.

10. Tour the client's facilities as they relate to the sales/service situation.

11. Get agreement on the goals and objectives of the project.

12. Prepare and disseminate a conference report that summarizes the relevant details of that meeting.

Using Advertising to continue our example: the A/E and the prospect can then develop and agree on a basic message they want to convey, and a project proposal from which all other programs and activities can be developed. For Consultative Selling the process is essentially the same, but the terminology may change depending upon the nature of the client's products or services. Once this part of the information-gathering/objective-setting process is complete, the work of the C/S has just begun. The C/S will then:

- Determine the team members within his or her organization who can best help achieve the client's objectives. Familiarize the team with a good summary of the information learned from the client.
- Follow up with the team to be sure they understand the wants, needs, goals and objectives of the client, and that the prep work is underway.

- Alert the client as to the progress that's being made and estimate a date for a follow-up meeting – then confirm the discussion by email or letter.
- By copies of memos, etc. let client know that your management is actively involved in the client's interests. One of the most-common reasons why firms lose clients – especially in the services industry – is because clients feel they aren't considered as important to the management as other of their clients.
- As the relationship develops, the C/S is alert to the actions needed to build the client's Respect and Trust – attending functions that relate to the client's business, attending sessions or seminars in which client or client members are involved, etc.
- Anticipate actions or events that may affect the client's project schedule, budget, etc, and advise the client in a timely, forthright manner.
- Don't promise more than your team or your firm can deliver.
- Upon completion of the team's work, arrange a meeting where the fruits of the project can be reviewed and hopefully approved.
- Using a conference report, communicate to all key influences the results of that meeting.
- Depending upon the situation, follow through as necessary, keeping contact and good relations with the client and other key influences.
- Maintain contact and relationships as appropriate, based on the nature of the client's future or continuing wants and needs.

- Without being obvious, try to ensure that the client's senior management and key influences are aware of your presence and involvement.
- Stay alert to opportunities to continue and enrich relationships, including ways to involve senior management of both companies in activities.
- Assure that clients get "Prompt Response to Needs and Requests
- Anticipate – or react promptly to – events or news, either good or bad, that occur and can involve the interests of the clients. The main purpose of this is to impress them that you are on top of the situation and have their interests at heart.
- Familiarize yourself with the Myers-Briggs testing process for determining social styles and personality. Take the test online. Know your own social style and familiarize yourself with an estimation of the others so you'll be better able to adjust to styles other than your own.
- Know when to say, "Yes." There will be occasions when you and the clients will not agree on the same solution to their problems. Remember: it's their problem and they have to live with it. Do your best to convince them, but if they insist, it's their problem – and their money.

Consultative Selling is more than a brand of behavior – it's an attitude. It's all about becoming a partner with your clients in order to help them solve their problems or improve their operations. As you can see from the number and variety of actions and considerations that are listed above – which may or may not be appropriate to your selling situation and will depend upon the nature or complexity of your product or service – there are many things to consider.

Life's Lessons Learned on Consultative Selling

"What's the real problem here?" When I was an Ad Agency Account Exec, I had a client who had trouble explaining the essence of the exact message he wanted to convey to prospects on promotional materials we were preparing. Rewriting headlines and ad copy – plus redoing layouts are expensive. So to be sure I'd have the message straight I developed a process that caused the client to really think the message through. I'd ask him to state the message in one sentence, sit there, write it out, and then ask him to review it. We'd do this a few times until he agreed with what he wanted to say.

I used to call that the "Basic Selling Proposition" and like to think that it was the forerunner to what became to be called the once-famous Positioning Statement (discussed in chapter six), which has now morphed into today's Value Proposition.

How much is too much?? One of the touchiest things that is often encountered in Consultative Selling is determining how much the prospects want to spend, or have budgeted for the product or service under consideration. Sometimes this is very clear; sometimes it's really difficult to discern – especially when services are involved.

In the advertising business – or other types of services – when you're dealing with prospects who have never advertised or used your type of service before, they'll often ask you to suggest a budget. To do the job right, the budget you suggest may shock them. My solution to this was to give them a range – low, medium, or high – then let them choose from there. It didn't work all the time, but most of the time, it did.

Several other case histories that are related to C/S are scattered elsewhere in this book. As you read them, you'll readily see how they relate to C/S and what the outcomes – both good and bad – were.

CHAPTER 11:
MISUSING THE BASICS OF SELLING

Throughout this book it's been assumed that anyone reading it is a senior manager or a Marketing-Sales professional – or at least is familiar with the ABCs of Sales and Marketing. Benefits; features; wants; and needs have been discussed before, but because these are so basic to Marketing-Sales, they're worth repeating:

1. A benefit is a desirable effect that a product or service produces for the user of that product or service. Saving money, improving quality and making things easier or better are some examples.

2. A feature is a good quality that enables the product or service to provide a benefit or satisfy a need. Faster operation, higher accuracy and greater reliability are examples of such features. Except in rare instances these should not be used as substitutes for benefits.

3. Wants and needs are the desires that any individual or group, who might be interested in any given product or service, might have. The wants & needs of end users will vary depending upon the product or service being considered (Chapter five). Of course, saving money or having a better ROI are pretty universal – as is prompt response to needs & requests.

Benefits that satisfy one or more major wants and needs should always be highlighted in the headlines or subheads of ads, presentations, sales materials, websites, etc. There are one or two exceptions to this rule. "A silly millimeter longer" was a very effective headline – despite it not referring to a benefit – but the product's outstanding feature made the emotional benefit so obvious, stating it was unnecessary. These situations, however, are rare. Speaking of ads, sales materials and websites, all of these should prominently display your logo, value proposition, plus a bid for action – and don't forget: Give the prospects an easy way to contact your company.

Other chapters have discussed the importance of identifying the few, top markets and types of prospects that account for the bulk of all sales to those markets, so more will not be said about it. That said, here are some selling basics that many salespeople don't seem to be aware of, or commonly ignore:

1. Salespeople are not the stars of the show, despite the fact that many of them think so. They're supposed to be the stage managers. It's their responsibility to create the climate and conditions that encourage the prospects to decide to buy from them. The prospects are the real the stars of the show.

2. Cold calling – dropping in on a prospect unannounced – is considered to be macho by many salespeople. Hence, cold calling is overemphasized and largely overrated. Cold calls are me-oriented and are often considered by the victim being called on as an intrusion on his or her time. Besides, cold calls rarely result in a sale, or an invitation to return to make another sales call later. Cold calling by phone has now become a necessary evil due to the demise of so many trade magazines. Perhaps Social Media will eventually obviate this irritant and expense.

3. Closing is also considered macho so most salespeople want to do it on every call. However, not every selling situation requires an overt sales pitch, or a need to "ask for the order." In many selling situations the objective of those doing the selling is to enhance their company's reputation by presenting research they have done, or discussing some award or special recognition they've received. Or the purpose of the call might be to recognize some contribution the customer has made for the good of the industry. In these cases restrain the urge – or break the unwritten rule that says every presentation requires that you ask for the order. When the objective is to enhance the reputation of the company – and your presentation succeeds at that – leave well enough alone. In these cases "asking for the order" most-often defeats the objective and harms your image.

Leave 'em wanting more

When I was with what was at the time New England's largest Ad Agency, a large, highly respected magazine publishing company visited us to present some important market research that they had conducted. The research was broad in scope and very much in-depth. The publishing company thought it was so important that three company VPs were involved in the presentation. All key buying influences and senior-management members of our Agency were in attendance – from the Chairman of the Board on down.

The presentation lived up to all that had been expected, and more. We were all very impressed – until the last few minutes. That's when the three VPs of the renowned publishing company went into a sales pitch about each of the magazines involved in the research.

It wasn't just me who lost respect for the publishing company. After the three VPs had left, every one of the Agency managers who had been in the room commented on how these publishing heavyweights had diminished their company's image because they slavishly hewed to the rule that says: "You're always supposed to ask for the order."

There are times when you should be satisfied that you've managed to impress a roomful of important prospects and buying influences.

Flying high...

Many years ago there was a joke about a flashing beacon on the top of a very tall tower. The story was that someone asked why the flashing beacon was up there. The answer was, "So planes won't accidentally fly into the tower." The follow-up question was, "What's the tower for?" The answer was, "To hold the flashing beacon up." Undue emphasis on "The Close" is a lot like the flashing beacon. Closing isn't all that tough if you build a good solid tower out of:

1. A thorough understanding of the prospect's wants and needs

2. A presentation that outlines the benefits you provide, which solve the prospects' wants & needs.

3. Demonstrate that you can reliably provide those benefits through a solid review of the features that enable you to provide those benefits.

4. Once you've done all that and answered all questions and concerns: then ask for the order.

Tom Sawyer was right.

When I was a National Sales Manager with a company that sold through distributors, I noticed that one of our salespeople had more sales than anyone else – not by a large amount, but he was still tops. He didn't boast about big orders he landed, or that he didn't bother with small accounts. Neither did he ignore the distributor salespeople who weren't focused on shooting elephants.

The secret to his success: He had a greater percentage of distributor reps selling for him than anyone else. Like Tom Sawyer, he had everyone wanting to pay him in order to paint the fence.

The moral: Don't let your ego get in the way of your success.

Telling isn't selling

This was mentioned before, but it's worth saying again: Listening is far more important than talking and schmoozing when you want to earn the respect and trust of your prospects – especially in the first meeting and the early stages of the business relationship. Even if you're responding to a prospect's inquiry, it's important to remember that prospects must first respect and trust you and your company before they'll be comfortable and confident in buying from you.

Don't just launch into the wonders of your product and all the benefits they'll get from it, try to learn their opinion of your product and your company. Ask them if they've had experience with the type of product you're selling and whether or not they've been satisfied. Next, determine if they've ever used your brand. If the answer is positive on both counts, that's great. If it isn't, explain how your company has improved things, and how you can help them.

After the call, follow up with a brief email thanking the prospects for their time and promise to send a letter that recaps the meeting. Prepare a letter that's both professional and grammatical, and send it out promptly. Then promptly follow up on that to see if there are any questions or comments. These demonstrations of "Prompt Response to Needs and Requests" help you in the first stage of earning those essentials to sales success – Respect and Trust.

Earning Respect

There are many cases where the fact that you're part of an illustrious company automatically gains you respect. Giant organizations often do that. So do smaller companies with great names: Rolls Royce, Ritz Carlton and Maxime's of Paris are a few such examples.

More often than not, you're going to be representing a company that doesn't have that degree of cachet. Either way, here are some things you should do to earn the Respect of your customers and prospects:

1. Know your product or service very well
2. Know the markets you're selling to
3. Know the wants & needs of your prospects and customers
4. Be a good Listener. Try to learn as much as you realistically can about the prospect's business.
5. Take good notes, and in most cases follow the session up with a complete conference report or letter that's free of errors in grammar and spelling
6. Be able to express and demonstrate how well your product or service satisfies those wants & needs
7. Know your competition

8. Know how to express your company's superiority over competition without being disrespectful of the competition

9. Be respectful of the time and attention your customers and prospects give you. Don't overstay your welcome.

10. Dress according to the sales situation. Some sources say you should dress on a par with, or one level above what the customer or prospect regularly wears.

11. Conduct yourself professionally, in accordance with the behavior of the customer or prospect

12. Remember: Prompt response to needs & requests is second in importance only to Low Price when all else is equal.

13. Also remember: Don't decline invitations to tour the customers' or prospects' facilities. That's like refusing to look at pictures of their kids.

14. Develop trust between you, the customer or prospect, and other important buying influences – both direct and indirect.

Developing Trust:

Trust is everything in a Sales relationship. This cannot be overemphasized. Earning someone's Trust doesn't happen overnight.

1. There's a simple formula for trust: Trust = Truth + Time.

2. Trust is gained by telling the truth – and keeping your word.

3. Keeping your word includes being there when you say you will, and doing what you said you'd do when you said you'd do it.

4. Don't promise more than you or your product can deliver.

5. Also remember: Prompt response to needs and requests is second only to low price in business situations when all else is equal. This cannot be repeated enough.

And always remember: Trust is fragile. It's very easily broken.

Chapter 12:
90% Firms Don't Have a Business Plan

This stunning statistic was recently reported by Time Warner. Considering that all start ups – those that are funded by outside sources, at least – must have a plan, this means that many established companies are selling by the seat of their pants.

If your company is part of that 90% and you want to get control of your sales and marketing activities, here are the ways to do it:

1. Ensure you know what markets best fit your products or services – are they high growth, mature, or in decline?
2. Be sure to include all key prospects – the top two or three categories that account for the large majority of your sales. If you're unsure of these:

- Consult with your top salespeople
- Use SEO or Social Media to learn through Analytics what their top wants and needs are
- Consult your competitors' websites to learn what they're emphasizing. Be careful not to emphasize those areas where they have superiority, or figure a way to improve your product or service

3. Don't forget to include those who indirectly influence the sale – a) dealers, b) people within the prospect organization who can be significant influences (in-house support staff: Maintenance, Executive Assistants, Senior Management, etc.), c) outside consultants (eg: Ad Agencies)

4. Develop a value proposition, and elevator pitch that succinctly states your superiority in satisfying those wants and needs – ensure it's short (25 words or less), powerful, and convincing
5. Develop – in writing, not just an outline – a brief Marketing-Sales plan that includes these elements:

   a) <u>Background/Situation:</u> Prepare a brief summary of your true business situation – your markets, the state of the markets, your position in the markets you serve, your methods of distribution, and all the conditions that can affect the future growth and profitability of the business. Be as forthright as possible. This is your business situation so it's important that it be thoroughly realistic.

   b) <u>Markets:</u> List all of the major markets that you serve and report on the state of each – are they high-growth, low-growth and mature, or in decline?

   c) <u>Prospects:</u> Who are the prospects that you serve? Ensure that you list them all – both direct and indirect. This itemization could help you identify market opportunities that are closely related to the ones you serve. As was stated earlier, sidestepping into related markets can usually be done with relatively little added effort and expense.

   d) <u>Competition:</u> Identify all the competitors in the markets you serve. Where possible, indicate the approximate market share of each, and whether your shares are increasing; and why.

   e) <u>Strengths:</u> Indicate the strengths of the products and services you provide relative to your competitors, and the degree of importance these strengths have from the standpoint of the prospects. It's important to remember that a relatively small advantage in a want or need that is highly important to your prospects will likely result in more sales than a strength in which you dominate the competition, but is not as important to the prospects.

f) Weaknesses: Repeat the same process you went through in identifying your relative strengths in order to accurately assess your relative weaknesses.

g) Opportunities and threats: As best you can, try to anticipate any opportunities or threats to your business that may exist, and estimate the impact they might have.

h) Objectives: List your objectives for the upcoming planning period. They should be realistic, affordable, achievable, and measurable.

i) Strategies: Itemize and describe the strategies you intend to pursue in order to achieve those objectives

j) Programs: Itemize and explain the programs you plan to undertake in order to successfully carry out those strategies.

k) Measurement: Indicate the methods you will use to evaluate the success or failure of these programs and strategies in relation to your objectives.

In preparing your business plan the best way to proceed is by creating an outline for each section, and then completing each section by writing your plan in detail. The detail you go through in doing this, forces you to think each situation through, and any contradictory conceptions or weaknesses will most likely become evident and you can rectify them.

Chapter 13:
Smart Start Ups and Product Launches

If you're involved in a start-up company and want to get financing from angels or venture capital firms, a thorough, airtight business plan is a must – just to get them to talk with you.

Even if you're independently wealthy, or have a rich uncle who'll back you all the way, don't omit the planning stage – if you know what's good for you, or your rich uncle. If you're introducing a totally new product for a going enterprise, chances are you'll be required to prepare a launch plan. On the off chance it's not required, do it anyway. The exercise will do you – and your prospects for a successful launch – a lot of good.

A good, solid plan will have about a dozen major sections and almost fifty sub-sections. Business plans for start-ups and product launches are complex and involve a lot of time, research and effort. I and a fellow founding partner recently collaborated on a business plan for a start-up venture and prepared a detailed plan. Together, we had well more than 800 hours invested in the project. Our plan conformed to standard formats, and included what most investors want to see. The sections and sub-sections we used are described later in this chapter, along with a description of the content that's needed.

Since there are far more failures caused by poor execution of the plan, we'll discuss "Working the Plan" before "Planning the Work."

Working the Plan

Execute the business plan as approved by your backers, and be prepared to make minor adjustments or adaptations as ensuing developments may require. You may want to have a pre-approved back-up plan in case foreseen but unlikely events make this necessary. Otherwise, alert your investors or corporate managers to get their agreement if other significant changes are needed.

Coordinate. Communicate. Cooperate. Evaluate.

<u>Coordinate:</u> Parts of your start-up/launch plan may only involve specific functions or departments. These should still be made known to all key players in order for everything and everybody to function as a unified whole. It's vital that the left hand know what the right hand is doing, both within the individual departments and without. For example:

1. Do the sales messages on your site or promotional campaigns dovetail with what your sales organization is saying?
2. If design and engineering have made any changes that affect costs or performance, do finance, sales and marketing, as well as your investors know about them?
3. If events are causing changes in the launch schedule does the whole team know about it?

<u>Communicate:</u> Startups and product launches are very dicey and everyone, including investors and corporate management, is very interested in the project. It's important that everyone be kept as current as possible on significant developments. Don't cover things up or gild the lily.

When it comes to new-product development and introduction, investors are usually more patient than corporate management in established companies. I've been involved in several corporate-funded new-product projects, as well as new business start-ups, and have found that the corporate patience level rarely extends beyond six months to a year, while investors will work with you for two years or more if they believe reasonable progress is being made and things are on the right track. This is not to say that corporate management will terminate the project, they'll just make the division involved in the project fund it themselves.

While investors are far more patient, don't lie to them or try to cover up problems or changes in direction. They'll pull the plug on you very quickly if they lose trust in what you say or do.

Cooperate: Teamwork is much more essential in a start-up or product launch than in other business situations. You don't yet have a strong, stable organization in place to provide a cushion for errors or omissions that arise because of a malcontent, grandstander or shirker. Also remember that full cooperation with requests made by investors or corporate management is vital to their maintaining confidence in you, the project and the team.

Evaluate: Have frequent staff meetings. Manage by walking around. Take the pulse of the project and the launch team frequently. Keep corporate management or your investors in the loop, but don't overdo it. Above all, instill confidence in everyone involved that the ship is on course and under the able command of the skipper.

Planning the Work:

A business plan – whether for a start-up company or a new-product launch – is no simple task. You need to cover all the bases, and research all the areas that impact your design, development, production, market development, selling, delivery, customer service, finance and administrative costs.

As you can see from the contents of a typical business plan, described below, there's a lot of detail involved. For a corporate-funded new-product launch you won't need to include sections on "The Company," "Management Team," "Management and Organization," and "Exit Strategy."

Executive Summary: While this is always the first part of the plan, it's nearly always written last. That's because you have to have the rest of the plan completed before you can write it intelligently and succinctly. By succinctly, I mean 3 or 4 pages or less – no exceptions. There will be a lot of key information packed into these two pages, and it may seem impossible to do in so few words – but it can and must be done.

Since a picture is worth a thousand words, I have included examples taken from a business plan I recently wrote to show how certain sections might be presented.

Mission Statement: The one we used was, "Utilize our unique pollutant-free air-conditioning technology to create a cleaner, more-livable environment by developing innovative products and systems that are eco-friendly, affordable and economical to operate."

System Description: Our invention was a system composed of four integrated components (products). If your invention is a single product or service, then the subtitle would be "Product Description" or "Service Description."

Disruptive Technology: Not every invention will have disruptive technology but if it does, that's a major point in your favor with investors. Emphasize this if you have it.

Products: Because our invention was a system and included four separate inventions and substantial innovations, it was to our advantage to describe them all:

1. "Our revolutionary new offset patio umbrella provides more headroom, plus ample space for installing a special ceiling fan to cool or warm the area beneath."

2. "The equally revolutionary Saf-T-Fan™ is a much safer alternative to conventional fans and its sales potential is worldwide – everywhere fans are used."

3. "Together they form a portable shelter to cool or warm table-sized, room-sized areas outdoors to increase comfort and greatly extend the use and revenue-generating capability of the facilities."

4. "Equipped with our patent-pending A/C technology, this system becomes 'The world's only portable one-piece shelter that air conditions or warms table-sized, room-sized areas outdoors – with no need for walls and without adding humidity."

Markets: Here you list the markets where your invention will have the greatest appeal to users. In our case the top market opportunities were:

1. Driving ranges and golf courses
2. Poolside and outdoor dining facilities at convention hotels and resorts
3. Upscale homes that have outdoor pools and other amenities
4. Sports venues and marinas that feature outdoor dining and entertainment areas
5. Camping, Homeland Security and the military
6. Replacements/Upgrades for areas using conventional fans

Future Products and Markets: Identify any products and market opportunities that you plan to have in the near or foreseeable future.

Industry Profile: Describe in general terms what industry the invention is part of – the more advanced the industry, or the better the long-term prospects for growth in that industry, the greater its appeal to investors.

The Company: This is a simple listing of the company's name, its location and the legal form of the business.

Management Team: Investors consider the quality and experience of the management team to be highly critical. It ranks up there with the invention itself. In addition to the key people who will have day-to-day responsibility for managing and operating the organization, the Board of Directors should also be listed, and the members should be executives that have excellent credentials in key areas of business. (It may be that some of the investors, themselves, will be on the Board.) Another area to include will be the recruitment and selection process to be used for hiring other key operating personnel.

Mission Statement: An example of what a mission statement might be is the one we developed for our startup: "Utilize our unique pollutant-free air-conditioning technology to create a cleaner, more-livable environment by developing and producing innovative products and systems that are eco-friendly, affordable and economical to operate."

The Products: Again, the definition of the new system, product or service should be stated. Examples of these definitions are listed in the "Executive Summary" section above. Intellectual property, if any, should also be explained here. This will include:
- Design data
- Disruptive technology (if any)

- Proof of concept

Features and Benefits: Features are good qualities inherent in the invention that enable the product or service to provide benefits for prospective users – those who have been reliably identified through market research. Benefits are solutions to proven, important end-user wants and needs that are satisfied through the acquisition and use of the product or service.

Marketing-Sales: This section should include the major markets you plan to address in the introduction of your system, product or service. It should also include your plans for the sales organization (direct sales, distributors, dealers, manufacturer's reps, etc.), as well as the sales message and media you intend to use in order to build your brand and convince prospects to buy your product. Here are the steps that you should undertake to accomplish this although not all of the details need to be included in the plan:

First, describe the major market segments that are known or believed to be top prospects for the product or service. Next, perform a positioning analysis (Chapter six) to determine and prioritize the most important wants and needs of those major prospects for your product or service. Based on this positioning analysis, a) Develop value propositions (Chapter six) that will most appeal to those key top-prospect groups. b) Identify the sales channels (Chapter five) that will enable you reach and serve those prospects. c) Outline the programs you plan to use that will attract and motivate these sales channels to sell your products. d) Briefly explain the promotional programs and website (Chapter seven) that will attract and motivate prospects to evaluate and purchase your products. e) Also include your plans to help assure customer satisfaction.

Direct/Indirect Competition: Include a full list of likely competitors – direct and indirect – as well as a description of these likely competitors, including their size and location.

SWOT Analysis: A detailed list of the company's strengths, weaknesses, opportunities and threats should be included as follows:
- Strengths of the product or service, relative to competition
- Weaknesses of the product or service relative to competition
- Opportunities – known, likely, and foreseeable
- Threats – known, likely, and foreseeable

Goals and Objectives: Be sure to include: a) projected sales in units and dollars, b) the markets to be developed, c) programs that will be implemented to achieve projected sales, prospect awareness and market penetration, d) other design, development, production and financial goals, e) programs that will be implemented to achieve those goals, and f) metrics that will indicate the degree of your success in meeting your goals and objectives.

Pricing: If there are no existing, comparable products or systems to help you estimate prices, other methods can be used to help you arrive at a reasonable value. When arriving at these "guesstimates," it's wise to have alternate pricing programs, such as quantity discounts, early-bird rates or special provisional pricing for beta-test sites. If, as said before, there is no comparable product or system to guide you, here are some pricing methods that are commonly used:

1. Cost to manufacture and distribute: Establish price based on this then assess market willingness to pay that price and adjust as necessary.
2. Through market research, determine what prospects are willing to pay; compare that to overall costs. (If volume will greatly

reduce cost, you might initially sell the product for a reduced profit in order to achieve those volumes very quickly.)

3. Package goods are often priced at about nine times the manufacturing cost plus packaging. (If the price is too high, try to cut costs to get pricing in line.)

4. Another formula: Manufacturing costs, plus R & D = forty-five percent of selling price.

<u>Projected Revenues:</u> Sales projections should be calculated on an estimate of unit demand, based on establishing market coverage, multiplied by the estimated selling price; plus any other revenues that might be generated by any variety of means – licensing, rentals, etc.

<u>Anticipated Growth:</u> An estimate of revenue growth based on the development of your launch markets, penetration of related markets, plus any added anticipated revenue based on expansion into other geographic areas.

<u>Selling and Promotional Costs:</u> These should include: a) commissions to salespeople, discounts to agents, distributors, etc. b) advertising and promotional costs – including website, brochures, advertising, newsletters, publicity, etc. c) travel and entertainment expenses d) tradeshow costs, including booth rental, cost of exhibit design and construction, shipping and set-up/knock-down charges, plus travel and expense for people who work the booth e) customer service and estimated costs of repair or service f) cost of returns.

<u>Production Costs:</u> Cost of parts or components, plus labor and overhead.

<u>Administrative Costs:</u> Salaries and bonuses for senior management and in-house personnel, plus costs for any outsourced services.

Financials: The financial summary should include all costs noted above, plus start-up costs, and research and development costs. These will be deducted from "Projected Revenues" as described above. Projected revenues should be listed in detail on a market-by-market basis, quarterly, for a period of at least three years. (Note: Investors will not expect this to be the exact outcome, but estimate as best you can so you can defend your projections if challenged.) These calculations will lead to "Anticipated Profits" (Losses) and help you forecast when the venture will become profitable and to what degree.

Exit Strategy: This should include: 1. Proposed methods for ways that investors can recoup their investment, plus profits. 2. The future of the company: a) continue to operate and expand, b) sell to prospective companies that might have interest now that the product has been proven.

Appendices: Depending upon the areas of the plan that require a more-detailed explanation to increase the plan's credibility and acceptance, the number of appendices will vary. These should be sufficiently thorough to give a satisfactory explanation of the situation. In our case we needed six appendices to explain our situation properly.

Passion – Prudence = Failure

A lot is said about an entrepreneur in a start-up company needing to have passion about the business, but not much is said about prudence or caution. No one's ever accused me of being overly cautious but I've been involved in, or observed, more start-up and product launch disasters because CEOs have not paid attention to what the market was telling them, or kept the investors properly informed. To me, there are two explanations for this:

1. The arrogance of ignorance

2. The ignorance of arrogance

I don't know which is worse, but they're both deadly.

In an earlier case history I cited, a person, who had been CFO for a large, well-known drug company, became our CEO. Being used to drug company profits, he decided that the scientific instruments divisions weren't profitable enough – even though profits equaled or exceeded industry averages, and sales accounted for about half the revenue of the entire company.

In an uninformed attempt to squeeze more profits out of the divisions, he brought in a whiz kid from a famous Fortune 50 company (a person who also didn't understand the business) to reorganize and streamline operations. (A major reorganization is as dicey and difficult as a start up or new-product launch.) After studying the situation for three or four months, the whiz kid decided that a "matrixed" organization would solve everything. Everything but serve the markets better, that is.

Despite what everyone was telling him he forged ahead blindly. Like the "Charge of the Light Brigade" or Lee's third day at Gettysburg, there were a lot of casualties from the debacle. The company sold half its business for fire-sale prices and many capable employees lost good-paying jobs.

The moral: Pay attention to what the market's telling you. "The customer (or investor) is most-often right."

Passion + Persistence = Profits

To close this discussion on an upbeat note, here's a real-life story with a happy ending – and proof that passion and persistence have their own rewards. When I was publisher of a trade magazine that reported on news and developments in industrial finishing, which includes all types of products (autos, trucks, refrigerators, washers, dryers – you name it), a new technology called "powder coating" arrived on the scene. It had some excellent features such as being better for the environment and easier to apply.

No one in the industry (except the powder people) thought or hoped this niche product would be broadly accepted. The industry association even declined to give powder coating a separate section in its product listings. But these up-start start-ups wouldn't take "no" for an answer. They fought and fought for recognition. Little by little users saw the advantages of powder. Today powder coating is the technology of choice by many in the industry.

The moral: New products and technologies have to fight for their place in the sun. Be passionate. Be persistent. It's the only way you'll win.

Chapter 14:
10 Remedies for the 10,000 Pitfalls to Start Ups and New-product Launches

Even for well-known, well-established companies new-product launches aren't easy. From the marketing standpoint, the most-serious mistakes are made while wearing rose-colored glasses when assessing the product's ability to satisfy the prospects' wants and needs. Because you're in love with the idea, you think everyone else will be, too.

When we introduced a new magazine focused exclusively on designers and builders of commercial buildings we were sure we had targeted a unique, un-served niche in a huge market, which was complemented by one of our magazines that was read by owners and managers of the same types of commercial buildings. We reasoned that this unmatched combination now gave advertisers access to all the important buying influences in the market, and that they would flock to this great combination. Putting their ads in these two publications would let them get their sales messages to all four major buying influences. We were right in some instances, but were rudely surprised in several others.

It turned out that when given a choice such as we offered, some advertisers decided that certain parts of their line were better suited to one group of readers rather than the other, and all we did was cause them to switch their advertising dollars from one magazine to the other. In other words, we created competition for ourselves in many cases, and now had the expense of publishing two magazines that failed to generate enough added revenue to offset the added investment. Our sin: We didn't remove those rose-colored glasses when we analyzed the opportunity.

Second on this perilous-pitfalls list are the compromises and trade-offs that often have to be made in product designs to trim costs to meet acceptable price points, or enhance one feature at the expense of another. A company I worked for was faced with that while developing a control system that would automate conventional machine tools. The market for these types of controls was very large and the demand for automated equipment was widespread and growing. All the trends were strongly in our favor, but there was just one problem: Design and development costs were getting out of hand. Engineering came up with a solution – or so they thought. The control as originally conceived called for two capabilities – point-to-point machining, and contouring. Contouring was normally used only ten percent of the time engineering reasoned, so let's eliminate the contouring feature and our costs will be back in line. There was just one problem: Contouring capability was like brakes on a car. They're used less than ten percent of the time, but you wouldn't buy a car that didn't have them. Needless to say, we dropped the project

Other highly common and major mistakes made by new-business planners include:

1. Overestimating the size of the market – both in units and in dollars. This is because: a) price lists usually overstate the true selling price of the products listed, b) figures from association data usually overstate the average size of the companies involved because a lot of smaller firms choose not to join associations for various reasons.

2. Failure to fully understand the markets. The magazine we launched for designers and builders of commercial buildings is

a good example. Another striking example is that million-dollar railroad-car identification fiasco that befell one of the world's largest and most-respected corporations, which was discussed in Chapter five.

Incorrectly Identifying the True Wants and Needs of the Prospects

The highly portable mini-spectrophotometer, also mentioned in Chapter five, which could be easily carried to lakes and ponds, is a perfect example of misreading the wants and needs of the market.

Failure to Properly and Precisely Develop a Value Proposition and Business Plan

Several ways to develop effective, persuasive value propositions this are explained in Chapter six. To repeat: Find a real and recognized need. a) Make very sure that the need is real and recognized. b) Don't rely solely on secondary (other people's) research. It's often wrong. c) Take off your rose-colored glasses – be hard-headedly realistic about your great, new product or service.

Next, prepare a compelling, airtight business plan (Chapters 12 and 13). Identify top markets and prospects by identifying the heavy users who can most benefit from your product or service. Remember, many markets and prospects prioritize their wants and needs differently, so learn each of them and tailor your message accordingly. Formulate a strong Value Proposition (Chapter six). A really good one will make your offering unique. To do this, remember:

a) Focus on the hot buttons of those few, key prospects.

b) Prospects buy benefits, not features (features prove your ability to deliver the benefits).

c) The best value propositions begin with "the only", should contain no more than twenty-five words and will trip off the tongue.

d) Use this Value Proposition as the core of all communications to prospects – elevator pitch, advertising, publicity, social media, website, promotional materials.

e) Use these extensively to build brand awareness and product interest among your prospects.

f) Remember: Branding is not a sometime thing (Chapter seven). It's a way of life – for life.

g) Branding is every public thing you do: packaging, users' manuals, customer service, correspondence, etc. (Chapter seven).

Optimize your ability to reach and serve your markets, customers and prospects. Manufacturers' representatives and distributors/dealers can greatly multiply the effectiveness of your sales force. Train and motivate them regularly to get best results – they have other lines to sell and you should view these lines as indirect competition.

Train your salespeople to think and act like stage managers – not stars of the show (Chapter 11). Establish a strong prospect-development program (Chapter eight). Don't stick sales with the job; they've got enough to do (Chapter ten).

Most importantly: Make "prompt response to customer-prospect needs and requests" job #1. Make sure it permeates your entire organization. It does no good if sales and customer service try to provide this, and others in your organization don't cooperate.

10 Remedies for the 10,000 Pitfalls to Start Ups and New-product Launches

Martial Arts Marketing

This two-part process outlines several steps that will help you improve and increase your market focus and develop a concise, strong, sharply focused sales message.

1. Identify those few, major segments that account for most market sales.

   Break down total market sales into major user groups. There are always a few groups of heavy users who account for most of the sales (Chapter five). Focus your efforts to be the best in meeting the wants and needs of the top two or three of these groups.

   Make sure you have included all key related influences (Chapter five). Dealers and distributors can be key segments, and are often overlooked, as are senior managers and key subordinates in your prospects' companies.

   Assess and factor in the growth potential of the various prospect groups. In the ceramics industry, for example, there are two distinct groups: traditional ceramics, which is in steep decline in the US – and advanced ceramics, which is very high in growth. Consider related markets where you can compete effectively. Sidestepping into related markets can usually be done with little added effort or expense.

   Situate your product so it's easy for prospects to find it, try it, and buy it. Conditions will vary from market to market – be sure to evaluate all options.

2. Determine that unique position that gives you dominance over competition.

Determine the likely responsiveness of these key segments to your ability to meet their major wants and needs vs. your competition (Chapters five and six). a) How well does your offering meet the special needs of users in these key segments? b) How well does it compare with competitors in these key segments?

Prioritize these key segments according to their suitability for your business situation: a) Do you have demonstrable advantages that will let you compete effectively in that market? b) Will your advantages let you compete successfully in the markets where the heavy users reside? c) Do you have the resources to compete effectively in that arena?

Bear in mind that a minor advantage in a benefit that is very important to your prospects will likely generate more sales than a major advantage in a benefit that is less important to your prospects (Chapter six). Walmart dominates its category by pricing lower than its competitors, even though quality and selection are largely the same, and its customer service is not always that good.

Chapter 15
15 Commandments for a Truly Integrated Marketing-Sales Process

1. List all your features that have user appeal
2. From among them, identify the benefits you can offer to various markets and prospects
3. Evaluate those markets to determine those that offer substantial revenue, growth and profit
4. Further analyze those markets to determine those 3 or 4 segments that have the greatest opportunity for long-term revenue, growth and profitability
5. For each of those few, key segments determine those top prospects who will likely have the greatest potential to influence the purchase of your products and services
6. Having selected those few, top buying-influence segments, prioritize their major wants and needs – the few that they most value and desire (some may be emotional, not rational)
7. From among these few, key desires, assess your ability to provide the ones you offer that are superior to the competition
8. Carefully and realistically determine your strengths and weaknesses vs. each competitor
9. Once you've determined the extent of your superiority over each competitor – plus your weaknesses, if any – determine

those segments in which you can best compete and prioritize those strengths accordingly

10. Having confirmed those areas where you can best compete – organize, direct and motivate your sales force (direct or indirect) to contact and convince those few, key prospects about your superiority

11. Develop a succinct (25 words or less), compelling Value Proposition that clearly sets you above and apart from the competition

12. Remember: a strength where you may have greater superiority over competition, but is not as highly desired by your prospects, may not generate as many sales as a strength where you have lesser superiority but is considered more important by these prospects

13. Establish and conduct a long-term Branding program that strongly and consistently conveys your Value Proposition. Avoid complicating it with less-persuasive details. Let the sales force handle them.

14. Assure the sales force is well versed in the Value Proposition, and that they know the need to educate and motivate those prospects who are most likely to be prime customers and repeat buyers

15. As new, important, proven developments come to light – no matter the source – incorporate them to assure that the Marketing-Sales process can promptly be adapted to changing conditions

www.ingramcontent.com/pod-product-compliance
Lightning Source LLC
Chambersburg PA
CBHW051706170526
45167CB00002B/555